Natalia Baena C

SPANISH
TO THE P◎INT

B1 VOCABULARY

- English ↔ Spanish
- Side-by-side translations
- Bilingual usage examples
- Includes IPA-based
  phonetic transcription

Spanish To The Point:
B1 Vocabulary

© 2021 Natalia Baena Cruces

Lead editor: Natalia Baena Cruces
Typesetting and publishing: Fluo Editions

ISBN: 979-8-52-181791-7

First edition: June 2021

Contents

Introduction

Vocabulary

Appendix

Introduction

Spanish To The Point: B1 Vocabulary pretende ser una herramienta útil y sencilla para todos aquellos estudiantes de español que deseen aumentar su vocabulario en esta lengua.

Se divide en doce unidades temáticas, cada una de las cuales incluye una completa lista de términos con su correspondiente traducción en inglés, acompañadas de oraciones en ambos idiomas. Asimismo, se incluye la transcripción fonética de todas las entradas según el Alfabeto Fonético Internacional (AFI).

Se trata de palabras seleccionadas especialmente para los candidatos de los exámenes DELE que buscan ampliar su léxico y perfeccionar su conocimiento del castellano.

Spanish To The Point: B1 Vocabulary aims to be a useful and simple companion aid for all Spanish students who wish to improve their vocabulary in this language.

It is divided into twelve thematic units, all of which include a complete list of terms with their corresponding translation in English, accompanied by sentences in both languages. For each and every one of the entries, you will also find the phonetic transcription according to the International Phonetic Alphabet (IPA).

The body of words in this book has been specifically selected for DELE exam candidates who seek to expand their vocabulary and improve their knowledge of Spanish.

N. Baena Cruz

Abbreviations

n	noun
v	verb
adj	adjective
adv	adverb
m	masculine
f	feminine

1 Household & Housework

acogedor/a *adj* • akoxeðor   **cosy**

Esta habitación es muy <u>acogedora</u>. ▸ This room is very <u>cosy</u>.

afueras *n, f* • afweras   **outskirts / suburb**

Su familia se mudó a una casa nueva en las <u>afueras</u> de la ciudad. ▸ His family moved into a new house in the <u>suburbs</u>.

aire acondicionado *n, m* • aire akondisjonaðo   **air conditioning**

Sólo usamos el <u>aire acondicionado</u> en agosto. ▸ We only use <u>air conditioning</u> in August.

alquilar *v* • alkilar   **to let / rent**

¿Puedo <u>alquilar</u> esta casa por unos meses? ▸ Can I <u>rent</u> this house for a few months?

alquiler *n, m* • alkiler   **hire / rent**

Como no podía pagar el <u>alquiler</u>, le pedí ayuda a él. ▸ Since I couldn't pay the <u>rent</u>, I asked him for help.

amplio/a *adj* • ampljo   **spacious / wide**

Quiero tener un salón amplio. ▸ I'd like to have a spacious living-room.

amueblado/a *adj* • amweβlaðo **furnished**

Estamos buscando un piso amueblado. ▸ We're looking for a furnished flat.

amueblar *v* • amweβlar **to furnish**

¿Cómo vais a amueblar vuestra casa? ▸ How are you going to furnish your new house?

ancho/a *adj* • aɲtʃo **wide / broad**

Hay una calle ancha cerca de mi casa. ▸ There is a wide street near my house.

ángulo *n, m* • Aŋgulo **angle / corner**

Ve las cosas desde todos los ángulos. ▸ She looks at things from all angles.

antiguo/a *adj* • antiɣwo **old / ancient**

Mi abuelo tiene un televisor antiguo que me quiere regalar. ▸ My grandfather has an old television that he wants to give me.

aparato *n, m* • aparato **device / appliance**

Quisiera pilas para este aparato. ▸ I would like batteries for this device.

aparcamiento *n, m* • aparkamjento **parking**

Le robaron el coche en ese aparcamiento. ▸ He had his car stolen in that parking lot.

apartamento *n, m* • apartamento **apartment**

8

Él vive solo en un apartamento. ▸ He lives alone in an apartment.

armario *n, m* • armarjo   **wardrobe / closet / cupboard**

Esta habitación tiene dos armarios para la ropa. ▸ This room has two closets for clothing.

ascensor *n, m* • asθensor, assensor   **lift / elevator**

Bajamos en el ascensor. ▸ We went down by elevator.

ático *n, m* • Atiko   **attic / penthouse**

Tom subió al ático por las escaleras. ▸ Tom climbed the stairs up to the attic.

avería *n, f* • aβerIa   **breakdown / failure**

¿Cuál fue la causa de la avería? ▸ What was the cause of the breakdown?

averiado/a *adj* • aβerjaðo   **broken**

Mi coche está averiado. ▸ My car has broken down.

azotea *n, f* • aθotea, asotea   **rooftop**

¿Qué estabas haciendo en la azotea? ▸ What were you doing on the rooftop?

balcón *n, m* • balkOn   **balcony**

Estoy en el balcón. ▸ I'm on the balcony.

baño *n, m* • baɲo   **bath / bathroom / restroom / toilet**

¿Dónde está el baño? ▸ Where is the bathroom?

barandilla *n, f* • baɾandiʎa   **banister / handrail / rail / railing**

María se inclinó sobre la barandilla. ▸ Maria leaned over the railing.

barrio *n, m* • baɾjo   **neighborhood**

En mi barrio hay un gran supermercado. ▸ There is a big supermarket in my neighborhood.

bien comunicado *adj* • bjen komunikaðo   **well connected**

¿Está tu barrio bien comunicado con el centro? ▸ Is your neighborhood well connected with the center?

bloque *n, m* • bloke   **block**

Vivo en ese bloque de pisos. ▸ I live in that block of flats.

buhardilla *n, f* • buaɾðiʎa   **garret / loft**

Llevo dos años viviendo en esta buhardilla. ▸ I've been living for two years in this loft.

calefacción *n, f* • kalefakθjOn, kalefaksjOn   **heating**

La calefacción no funciona. ▸ The heating doesn't work.

calentar *v* • kalentaɾ   **to heat**

¿Podrías calentar este plato? ▸ Could you heat this dish?

casero/a *adj* • kaseɾo   **home-made / home-loving**

Sin duda soy una persona casera. ▸ I'm definitely a home-loving person.

cemento *n, m* ● θemento, semento   **cement**

El cemento fraguará en un par de horas. ▸ The cement will set in a couple of hours.

chalé *n, m* ● tʃalE   **villa / detached house**

Me encantaría vivir en un chalé. ▸ I'd love to live in a villa.

clásico/a *adj* ● klAsiko   **classic / classical / vintage**

Algunas personas compran muebles clásicos. ▸ Some people buy classic furniture.

coche *n, m* ● kotʃe   **car**

Ninguno de los coches es mío. ▸ None of the cars is mine.

comedor *n, m* ● komeðor   **dining room / dining area**

Nuestra casa tiene siete habitaciones, incluyendo el comedor. ▸ Our house has seven rooms including the dining room.

comunidad *n, f* ● komuniðað   **community**

Los grupos son un buen medio para compartir intereses con una pequeña comunidad o el mundo entero. ▸ Groups are a good way to share an interest with a small community or the whole world.

conexión a internet *n, f* ● koneksjOn a internet   **internet connection**

Tengo una buena conexión a internet. ▸ I have a good internet connection.

conserje *n, m* ● konserxe   **caretaker / concierge / janitor**

Soy el conserje de este edificio. ▸ I'm the caretaker of this building.

construcción *n, f* • konstrukθ/sjOn   **building / construction**

¿Cuánto dinero se ha gastado en la construcción del museo? ▸ How much money has been spent on building the museum?

corte *n, m* • korte   **cutoff**

¿Cuánto va a durar el corte de luz? ▸ How long is the cutoff of the electricity going to last?

cristal *n, m* • kristal   **crystal / glass**

El cuenco de cristal se rompió en trozos diminutos. ▸ The glass bowl broke into tiny fragments.

cuarto *n, m* • kwarto   **bedroom / room**

Mary está estudiando en su cuarto. ▸ Mary is studying in her room.

dar de alta *v* • dar de alta   **to sign up**

Cuando te mudes a tu nueva casa, tendrás que dar de alta servicios como la electricidad. ▸ When you move to your new home, you will have to sign up for services like electricity.

dar de baja *v* • dar de baxa   **to disconnect / to shut off**

¿Por qué la empresa de electricidad dio de baja el servicio? ▸ Why did the electricity company disconnect the service?

decoración *n, f* • dekoraθjOn, dekorasjOn   **decoration**

Él estudió decoración de interiores. ▸ He studied interior decoration.

delante prep • delante **in front**

Espero que nadie se siente delante de nosotros. ▸ I hope no one sits in front of us.

derecha n, f • deɾetʃa **right**

La carretera se curva hacia la derecha en este punto. ▸ The road bends sharply to the right at this point.

desorden n, m • desoɾðen **mess / disorder**

¿Eres tú el responsable de este desorden? ▸ Are you responsible for this mess?

desordenado/a adj • desoɾðenaðo **messy / untidy**

Su cuarto está desordenado. ▸ His room is untidy.

desordenar v • desoɾðenaɾ **to make a mess / untidy**

¿Es que tienes que desordenarlo todo cada día? ▸ Do you need to make a mess every day?

despacho n, m • despatʃo **office / study**

Creo que Tom está en su despacho. ▸ I think Tom is in his office.

desperfecto n, m • despeɾfekto **damage / flaw**

Tengo que pagar los desperfectos. ▸ I have to pay for the damages.

detrás prep • detɾAs **behind**

13

Hay un jardín elegante <u>detrás</u> del palacio. ▸ There's an elegant garden be-<u>hind</u> the palace.

diminuto/a *adj* • diminuto   **tiny**

Viven en un apartamento <u>diminuto</u>. ▸ They live in a <u>tiny</u> apartment.

edificio *n, m* • eðifiθjo, eðifisjo   **building**

El banco tiene una hipoteca sobre su <u>edificio</u>. ▸ The bank holds a mortgage on his <u>building</u>.

electricidad *n, f* • elektriθiðað, elektrisiðað   **electricity / power**

Ella apagó la luz para no desperdiciar <u>electricidad</u>. ▸ She turned out the light so as not to waste <u>electricity</u>.

eléctrico/a *adj* • elEktriko   **electric / electrical**

Este reloj es <u>eléctrico</u>. ▸ This clock is <u>electric</u>.

empresa de mudanzas *n,f* • empresa de muðansas **removal company / moving company**

¿Podrías darme el teléfono de la <u>empresa de mudanzas</u>? ▸ Could you give me the <u>moving company</u> telephone number?

empresa de transporte *n, f* • empresa de transporte **transport company / shipping company**

Estoy muy satisfecho con esta <u>empresa de transportes</u>. ▸ I'm very satisfied with this <u>shipping company</u>.

enorme *adj* • enorme   **enormous / huge**

Ella vive en una casa enorme. ▸ She lives in a huge house.

ensuciar v • ensuθjar, ensusjar   **to get dirty**

La cocina se ensucia fácilmente. ▸ The kitchen gets dirty easily.

entrada n, f • entraða   **entrance / hall**

Ella vio un joven en la entrada. ▸ She saw a young man at the entrance.

escalera n, f • eskalera   **stairs / ladder**

Ten cuidado con donde pisas cuando bajes la escalera. ▸ Watch your step in going down the stairs.

escritorio n, m • eskritorjo   **desk**

Este escritorio es un poco bajo para mí. ▸ This desk is a little low for me.

espacio n, m • espaθjo, espasjo   **space / room**

Debes hacer espacio para el televisor. ▸ You must make room for the television.

espacio verde n, m • espasjo berðe   **green space**

Cada vez hay menos espacios verdes en la ciudad. ▸ There are fewer and fewer green spaces in the city.

espacioso/a adj • espaθjoso, espasjoso   **spacious**

Este auto es espacioso y práctico. ▸ This car is spacious and practical.

establecerse v • estaβleθerse, estaβleserse   **to settle**

¿Cuándo se establecieron en esta región? ▸ When did they settle in this re-

15

gion?

estrecho/a *adj* • estreʧo **narrow**

Caminaron por un sendero estrecho. ▸ They walked along a narrow path.

estudio *n, m* • estuðjo **study / studio**

El estudio es muy pequeño, sin lugares donde esconderse. ▸ The studio is very small, with no place to hide.

exterior *adj* • eksterjor **exterior / outside**

El exterior de la casa estaba muy deteriorado. ▸ The outside of the house was very run down.

factura *n, f* • faktura **bill / invoice**

La factura debe ser pagada hoy. ▸ The bill must be paid today.

fianza *n, f* • fjanθa, fjansa **deposit / bail**

¿Pagaste la fianza? ▸ Did you pay the deposit?

fontanería *n, f* • fontanerˈia **plumbing**

No sé nada de fontanería. ▸ I know nothing about plumbing.

fontanero *n, m* • fontanero **plumber**

Si tú no puedes arreglar la tubería, tendremos que llamar a un fontanero. ▸ If you can't fix the pipe, we'll have to call a plumber.

fregar *v* • freɣar **to wash**

Ella acaba de <u>fregar</u> los platos. ▸ She has just finished <u>washing</u> dishes.

funcional *adj* • funθjonal, funsjonal   **functional**

Prefiero tener un mobiliario <u>funcional</u>. ▸ I prefer to have <u>functional</u> furniture.

funcionar *v* • funθjonar, funsjonar   **to work / to operate**

¿Podría explicarnos cómo <u>funciona</u> el lavavajillas? ▸ Could you explain how the dishwasher <u>works</u>?

garaje *n, m* • garaxe   **garage**

La bicicleta de los chicos está en el <u>garaje</u>. ▸ The boys' bicycle is in the <u>garage</u>.

gas natural *n, m* • gas natural   **natural gas**

¿Usas <u>gas natural</u> para calentar tu casa? ▸ Do you use <u>natural gas</u> to heat your house?

gastos del hogar *n, m* • gastos del oyar   **household expenses**

¿Quién paga los <u>gastos del hogar</u>? ▸ Who pays the <u>household expenses</u>?

grande *adj* • grande   **big / large**

Mi habitación es dos veces más <u>grande</u> que la de él. ▸ My room is twice as <u>big</u> as his.

grifo *n, m* • grifo   **tap / faucet**

El agua mineral es, por lo general, más cara que el agua del <u>grifo</u>. ▸ Generally, mineral water is more expensive than tap water.

habitación *n, f* • aβitaθjOn, aβitasjOn   **bedroom / room**

Esta habitación lleva vacía mucho tiempo. ▸ The room has been empty for a long time.

habitual *adj* • aβitwal   **habitual / usual**

Tom y Mary se sentaron a cenar a la hora habitual. ▸ Tom and Mary sat down to dinner at the usual time.

hierro *n, m* • jero   **iron**

El hierro es duro. ▸ Iron is hard.

hipoteca *n, f* • ipoteka   **mortgage**

Mi casa no tiene hipoteca. ▸ My house is a mortgage-free house.

hormigón *n, m* • ormiɣOn   **concrete**

Este edificio está hecho de hormigón armado. ▸ This building is made of reinforced concrete.

hueco *n, m* • weko   **gap / hole**

Cuidado, hay un hueco en el piso. ▸ Be careful. There's a hole in the floor.

impresionante *adj* • impresjonante **breathtaking / impressive / striking**

Su casa tiene unas vistas impresionantes. ▸ Her house has a breathtaking view.

incomodidad *n, f* • iŋkomoðiðað   **discomfort / inconvenience**

No me gusta la incomodidad de este lugar. ▸ I don't like the discomfort of this place.

incómodo/a *adj* • iŋkOmoðo   **uncomfortable**

El sofá es incómodo. ▸ The sofa is uncomfortable.

inmobiliaria *n, f* • immoβiljaɾja   **real state agency**

Esta agencia inmobiliaria vendió mi casa. ▸ This real estate agency sold my house.

inquilino/a *n, m/f* • iŋkilino   **tenant**

Nunca he tenido problemas con mis inquilinos. ▸ I've never had problems with my tenants.

instalación *n, f* • instalaθjOn, instalasjOn   **installation / facility**

Quiero poner una instalación geotérmica. ▸ I would like to set up a geothermal installation.

instalar *v* • instalaɾ   **to install**

El hombre trató de instalar su propia antena. ▸ The man tried to install his own antenna.

interior *adj* • inteɾjoɾ   **inner / inside / interior / internal**

Estas cajas tienen mucho espacio en su interior. ▸ These boxes have plenty space inside.

izquierda *n, f* • iθkjeɾða, iskjeɾða   **left**

Abre el armario de la izquierda, allí están las botellas. ▸ Open the cupboard to the left, the bottles are in there.

lavadero *n, m* • laβaðero   **sink / laundry room**

¿Puedes poner esta ropa en el lavadero? ▸ Can you put these clothes in the laundry room?

limpiar *v* • limpjar   **to clean**

Tengo que limpiar mi habitación. ▸ I have to clean my room.

limpieza *n, f* • limpjeθa, limpjesa   **cleanup / cleaning**

Hoy tengo que hacer la limpieza. ▸ I have to do the cleaning today.

limpieza a fondo *n, f* • limpjeθa/limpjesa a fondo   **deep cleaning**

Esta habitación necesita una limpieza a fondo. ▸ This room needs deep cleaning.

limpio/a *adj* • limpjo   **clean / neat**

¿Me podrías traer un cuchillo limpio, por favor? ▸ Could you please bring me a clean knife?

llenar *v* • ʎenar   **to fill**

¿Por qué has llenado la casa de estas cosas? ▸ Why did you fill the house with this stuff?

local *n, m* • lokal   **local / premises**

¿Eres miembro de tu biblioteca local? ▸ Are you a member of your local library?

luminoso/a *adj* • luminoso   **bright / light**

¡Qué día tan luminoso! ► What a bright day!

luz n, f • luθ, lus   **light**

En esta habitación no hay suficiente luz para coser. ► There's not enough light in this room for sewing.

madera n, f • maðera   **wood**

El juguete está hecho de madera. ► That toy is made of wood.

mantener v • mantener   **to keep / to maintain**

Es difícil mantener limpias las alfombras blancas. ► White carpets are very hard to keep clean.

máquina n, f • mAkina   **car / machine**

El ingeniero nos dijo cómo usar la máquina. ► The engineer told us how to use the machine.

mascota n, f • maskota   **mascot / pet**

Ella me dijo que quería un perro de mascota. ► She told me that she wanted a pet dog.

material n, m • materjal   **material / fabric**

¿Es un buen material? ► Is it a good material?

mecánico/a adj/n • mekAniko   **machinist / mechanic / mechanical**

Este juguete es mecánico. ► This is a mechanical toy.

mecedora n, f • meθeðora, meseðora   **rocking chair**

Recuerdo la mecedora de mi abuela. ▸ I remember my grandma's rocking chair.

minimalista *adj* • minimalista   **minimal / minimalist**

El es un artista minimalista muy famoso. ▸ He is a very famous minimalist artist.

mobiliario *n, m* • moβiljarjo   **furniture**

Ella amuebló la habitación con un precioso mobiliario. ▸ She furnished the room with beautiful furniture.

moderno/a *adj* • moðerno   **modern**

Los muebles del salón eran de estilo moderno. ▸ The living room furniture was modern in style.

mudanza *n, f* • muðanθa, muðansa   **move / relocation / removal**

¿Puedes ayudarnos con la mudanza? ▸ Can you help us with the move?

mueble *n, m* • mweβle   **furniture**

Ese mueble es de mi madre. ▸ That furniture is my mother's.

muro *n, m* • muɾo   **wall**

No te subas al muro. ▸ Don't climb up the wall.

objeto *n, m* • oβxeto   **object**

¿Hay algún líquido u objetos punzantes en tu equipaje? ▸ Are there any liquids or sharp objects in your luggage?

obra *n, f* • oβɾa   **work / construction / job**

Falta poco para terminar las obras de construcción. ▸ The construction work is steadily nearing completion.

obrero *n, m* • oβrero   **hand / laborer / worker**

El obrero está cargando arena con una pala. ▸ The worker is carrying sand with a shovel.

oficina *n, f* • ofiθina, ofisina   **agency / bureau / office**

Nuestra oficina está en la parte norte del edificio. ▸ Our office is on the northern side of the building.

orden *n, m/f* • orðen   **order**

Aquí está todo en orden. ▸ Everything's in order here.

ordenado/a *adj* • orðenaða   **ordered / organized / tidy**

Lo reconozco, no soy la persona más ordenada del mundo. ▸ I admit, I'm not the tidiest person in the world.

ordenar *v* • orðenar   **to organize / to tidy up / to order**

¿Podrías ordenar tu cuarto? ▸ Could you tidy up your room?

orientación *n, f* • orjentaθjOn, orjentasjOn   **guidance / orientation**

¿Cuál es la orientación de tu nueva casa? ▸ What's the orientation of your new house?

oscuridad *n, f* • oskuriðað   **dark / darkness**

Él estaba buscando algo en la oscuridad. ▸ He was looking for something in the <u>dark</u>.

oscuro/a *adj* • oskuro   **dark**

Esta habitación está demasiado <u>oscura</u>. ▸ This room is too <u>dark</u>.

panorama *n, m* • panorama   **panorama / outlook**

Me encanta el <u>panorama</u> desde esta colina. ▸ I love the <u>panorama</u> from this hill.

pasar la aspiradora *v* • pasar la aspiraðora   **to hoover / to vacuum**

¿Puedes <u>pasar la aspiradora</u> en el salón? ▸ Can you <u>vacuum</u> the living room?

pasillo *n, m* • pasiʎo   **corridor / aisle**

Nos acabamos de encontrar en el <u>pasillo</u>. ▸ We just met in the <u>corridor</u>.

patio *n, m* • patjo   **court / courtyard / patio / yard**

Solía haber un jardín en nuestro <u>patio</u>. ▸ There used to be a garden in our <u>yard</u>.

pestillo *n, m* • pestiʎo   **latch / bolt**

Tenemos que arreglar el <u>pestillo</u> inmediatamente. ▸ We have to fix the <u>latch</u> immediately.

piscina *n, f* • pisθina, pissina   **swimming pool**

Está nadando en la <u>piscina</u>. ▸ He is <u>swimming</u> in the pool.

piso *n, m* • piso   **flat / floor / apartment**

Estoy ocupado buscando piso. ▸ I'm busy looking for an apartment.

piso compartido *n, m* • piso kompartiðo **shared flat / shared apartment**

¿Es verdad que vives en un piso compartido? ▸ Is it true that you live in a shared flat?

planta *n, f* • planta   **floor / plant**

Vivo en la planta baja. ▸ I live on the ground floor.

portal *n, m* • portal   **hallway / entrance hall**

Estamos esperándote en el portal. ▸ We are waiting for you in the hallway.

portero *n, m* • portero   **doorman**

¿Puedes hacerme el favor de avisar al portero de que el ascensor no funciona? ▸ Could you do me the favor of telling the doorman the elevator doesn't work?

portero electrónico *n, m* • portero elektroniko   **intercom**

No escuché el portero electrónico. ▸ I didn't hear the intercom.

práctico/a *adj* • praktiko   **handy / practical**

Es muy práctico. ▸ That's very handy.

propietario/a *n, m/f* • propjetarjo   **owner**

¿Es usted el propietario de esta casa? ▸ Are you the owner of this house?

puerta blindada *n, f* • pwerta blindaða   **reinforced door**

25

No necesitamos una puerta blindada. ▸ We don't need a reinforced door.

recargado/a *adj* • rekarɣaðo   **excessively ornate / overloaded**

¿No crees que esta habitación está un poco recargada? ▸ Don't you think this room is excessively ornate?

reforma *n, f* • reforma   **remodeling / reform**

Estoy de reforma. ▸ I'm remodeling.

reformar *v* • reformar   **to remodel / to reform**

¿Por qué quieres reformar toda la casa? ▸ Why do you want to remodel the whole house?

renta *n, f* • renta   **rent / income**

Estoy buscando una casa en renta. ▸ I am looking for a house to rent.

reparar *v* • reparar   **to fix / to repair / to mend**

No puedo reparar la computadora. ▸ I can't repair the computer.

resistente *adj* • resistente   **resistant / strong / tough**

Este material es muy resistente. ▸ This material is very strong.

ropa *n, f* • ropa   **clothes / clothing**

Su ropa está gastada. ▸ His clothes are worn out.

sala *n, f* • sala   **sitting room / room / venue**

La dejaron sola en la sala. ▸ She was left alone in the room.

secar *v* • sekaɾ   **to dry**

Nunca vas a secar la ropa si la dejas bajo la sombra. ▸ You are never going to dry the clothes if you leave them in the shade.

seco/a *adj* • seko   **dry**

Guarde en un lugar fresco y seco. ▸ Store in a cool and dry place.

seguridad *n, f* • seɣuɾiðað   **safety / security**

Ella está preocupada por tu seguridad. ▸ She's worried about your safety.

sencillo *adj* • senθiʎo, sensiʎo   **simple / plain**

Me gustan las cosas sencillas. ▸ I like simple things.

silla *n, f* • siʎas   **chair**

Estas sillas son diferentes. ▸ These chairs are different.

sillón *n, m* • siʎOn   **armchair / couch**

No deja que nadie se siente en su sillón. ▸ He won't let anybody sit in his armchair.

sonido *n, m* • soniðo   **sound**

Usted puede escuchar el sonido del mar en esta habitación de hotel. ▸ You can hear the sound of the sea in this hotel room.

sótano *n, m* • sOtano   **basement / cellar**

El arpa vieja estaba guardada en el sótano. ▸ The old harp was stored in the basement.

suciedad *n, f* • suθjeðað, susjeðað — dirt / filth

El jabón ayuda a eliminar la suciedad. ▸ Soap helps remove the dirt.

sucio/a *adj* • suθjo, susjo — dirty / filthy

A él no le importa si su auto está sucio. ▸ He doesn't care if his car is dirty.

suelo *n, m* • swelo — floor / ground

Hagan un círculo en el suelo. ▸ Make a circle on the floor.

tareas domésticas *n, f* • taɾeas domEstikas — housework

¿Necesitas ayuda con las tareas domésticas? ▸ Do you need help with the housework?

techo *n, m* • tetʃo — ceiling / roof

Él no era lo suficientemente alto como para llegar al techo. ▸ He wasn't tall enough to get at the ceiling.

técnico *n/adj* • tEkniko — technical / technician

Necesitas conocimiento técnico para entender cómo funciona este sistema. ▸ You need technical knowledge to understand how this system works.

tejado *n, m* • texaðo — roof / rooftop

El pájaro que hay sobre el tejado es un cuervo. ▸ The bird on the roof is a crow.

teléfono fijo *n, m* • telEfono fixo — landline

No, no tengo teléfono fijo. ▸ No, I don't have a landline.

tendedero *n, m* • tendeðeɾo   **clotheshorse / clothesline**

Colgué la manta en el tendedero. ▸ I hung the blanket on the clothesline.

tender *v* • tendeɾ   **to hang up / to hang out**

Voy a tender la ropa. ▸ I'm going to hang the clothes.

terraza *n, f* • teraθa, terasa   **balcony / terrace**

Una pareja de gorriones está construyendo un nido en la terraza de mi casa.
▸ A couple of sparrows are building a nest on the balcony of my house.

timbre *n, m* • timbɾe   **doorbell**

Sonó el timbre de la puerta. ▸ The doorbell rang.

trastero *n, m* • trasteɾo   **storage room**

Hay demasiadas cosas en el trastero. ▸ There are too many things in the storage room.

tubería *n, f* • tuβeɾía   **pipe / pipeline**

Tú puedes oír el goteo del agua por la tubería. ▸ You can hear the water dripping from the pipe.

ubicación *n, f* • uβikaθjOn, uβikasjOn   **location**

Esta es la ubicación perfecta. ▸ This is the perfect location.

urbanización *n, f* • uɾβaniθaθjOn, uɾβanisasjOn   **residential area**

Nunca he estado en esta urbanización. ▸ I've never been in this residential area.

uso *n, m* • uso   **use**

Todo esto es para mi uso personal. ▸ All this is for my personal use.

vecindario *n, m* • beθindarjo, besindarjo   **neighborhood**

Ha habido una oleada de robos en mi vecindario. ▸ There has been a rash of burglaries in my neighborhood.

vecino/a *n, m/f* • beθino, besino   **neighbor**

Es nuestra vecina. ▸ She is our neighbor.

vestíbulo *n, m* • bestíβulo   **lobby / hall**

Te veo en el vestíbulo a las tres. ▸ I'll meet you in the lobby at three.

vista *n, f* • bista   **view**

Me gustaría tener un cuarto con buenas vistas. ▸ I'd like to have a room with a nice view.

vivienda *n, f* • biβjenda   **house / housing**

Estoy delante de tu vivienda. ▸ I'm in front of your house.

2 Food & Cooking

aceite *n, m* • aθeite, aseite   **oil**

Él compró un montón de harina y de aceite. ▸ He bought a lot of flour and oil.

aceite de girasol *n, m* • aseite de xirasol   **sunflower oil**

¿Alguna vez usas aceite de girasol? ▸ Do you ever use sunflower oil?

aceite de oliva *n, m* • aseite de oliβa   **olive oil**

Normalmente cocino con aceite de oliva. ▸ I usually cook with olive oil.

aceitoso/a *adj* • aθeitoso, aseitoso   **oily**

No me gusta la comida aceitosa. ▸ I don't like oily food.

aceituna *n, f* • aθeituna, aseituna   **olive**

Me encantan las aceitunas verdes. ▸ I love green olives.

ácido/a *adj* • Aθiðo, Asiðo   **acid**

La vitamina C también es conocida como ácido ascórbico. ▸ Vitamin C is also known as ascorbic <u>acid</u>.

adelgazamiento *n, m* • aðelgaθamjento, aðelgasamjento   **weight loss**

¿Qué ha causado tu <u>adelgazamiento</u>? ▸ What caused your <u>weight loss</u>?

adelgazar *v* • aðelgaθaɾ, aðelgasaɾ   **to lose weight**

Ella está intentando <u>adelgazar</u>. ▸ She is trying to <u>lose weight</u>.

agitar *v* • axitaɾ   **to shake**

<u>Agitar</u> antes de usar. ▸ <u>Shake</u> before using.

agregar *v* • aɣɾeɣaɾ   **to add**

Debe <u>agregar</u> una cucharadita de azúcar. ▸ You must <u>add</u> a teaspoon of sugar.

agrio/a *adj* • aɣɾjo   **sour**

La leche tiene un sabor <u>agrio</u>. ▸ Milk tastes <u>sour</u>.

al punto *adv* • al punto   **medium**

¿Le gustaría cocinado <u>al punto</u>? ▸ Would you like it to be cooked <u>medium</u>?

alergia *n, f* • aleɾxja   **allergy**

¿Sufre de <u>alergias</u> estacionales? ▸ Do you suffer from seasonal <u>allergies</u>?

alérgico/a *adj* • alEɾxiko   **allergic**

Él es alérgico al polvo. ▸ He is allergic to dust.

almuerzo n, m • almweɾθo, almweɾso   **dinner / lunch**

¿Qué tal si damos un paseo después del almuerzo? ▸ How about going for a walk after lunch?

amargo/a adj • amaɾγo   **bitter**

Este café está amargo. ▸ This coffee tastes bitter.

anorexia n, f • anoɾeksja   **anorexia**

Tuvo anorexia cuando era joven. ▸ She suffered from anorexia when she was young.

anoréxico/a adj • anoɾEksiko   **anorexic**

Está tan delgado que pensé que era anoréxico. ▸ He is is thin that I thought he was anorexic.

antioxidante n, m • antjoksiðante   **antioxidant**

¿Sabías que esta vitamina es un fantástico antioxidante? ▸ Did you know this vitamin is a great antioxidant?

añadir v • aɲaðiɾ   **to add**

Creo que deberías añadir un poco más de pimienta. ▸ I think that you should add a little more pepper.

apetito n, m • apetito   **appetite**

Tengo poco apetito. ▸ I have little appetite.

arándano n, m • aɾAndano   **blueberry / bilberry / cranberry**

33

Su torta de arándano azul estaba deliciosa. ▸ The blueberry cake he made was delicious.

asar *v* • asaɾ **to grill / to roast**

Vamos a asar las castañas. ▸ Let's roast the chestnuts.

atún *n, m* • atUn **tuna**

Me comí una ensalada de atún. ▸ I ate a tuna salad.

ayuno *n, m* • ajuno **fasting**

El ayuno no es para mí. ▸ Fasting is not for me.

azúcar *n, f/m* • aθUkaɾ, asUkaɾ **sugar**

Se vende azúcar en la tienda. ▸ They sell sugar at the store.

azucarado/a *adj* • aθukaɾaðo, asukaɾaðo **sugary / sweet**

Esta bebida está azucarada. ▸ This drink is sweet.

basura *n, f* • basuɾa **garbage / trash / rubbish / litter**

¿Dónde ponéis la basura en esta cocina? ▸ Where do you put the garbage in this kitchen?

batidora *n, f* • batiðoɾa **blender / mixer**

Ella compró una tostadora, una cafetera, un hervidor de huevos y una batidora de mano. ▸ She bought a toaster, a coffeemaker, an egg cooker and a hand mixer.

batir *v* • batiɾ **to beat / to whip / to whisk**

¿Vas a usar la batidora para batir los huevos? ► Are you going to use the blender to beat the eggs?

bebida *n, f* ● beβiða | **beverage / drink**

Usted pronto vendrá a disfrutar de la comida y la bebida aquí. ► You'll soon come to enjoy the food and drink here.

bizcocho *n, m* ● biθkotʃo, biskotʃo | **sponge cake**

Es el mejor bizcocho que he comido. ► It's the best cake I've ever eaten.

bollería *n, f* ● boʎerɪa | **pastries / baked goods**

¿Dónde está la sección de bollería? ► Where's the baked goods section?

bulimia *n, f* ● bulimja | **bulimia**

La bulimia es un trastorno de la alimentación. ► Bulimia is an eating disorder.

bulímico/a *adj* ● bulɪmiko | **bulimic**

¿Tienes algún síntoma bulímico? ► Do you have any bulimic symptom?

calabacín *n, m* ● kalaβaθɪn, kalaβasɪn | **courgette / zucchini**

¿A ti te gusta el calabacín? ► Do you like zucchini?

calentar *v* ● kalentar | **to heat**

¿Podrías calentar este plato? ► Could you heat this dish?

calidad *n, f* ● kaliðað | **quality**

35

Prefiero calidad a cantidad. ► I prefer quality to quantity.

caliente *adj* • kaljente   **hot / warm**

¿Quién quiere chocolate caliente? ► Who wants some hot chocolate?

calor *n, m* • kalor   **heat / hot / warmth**

Se dice que hará mucho calor. ► They say it will be very hot.

calórico/a *adj* • kalOriko   **caloric**

Las bebidas refrescantes suelen tener un alto contenido calórico. ► Carbonated beverages oftentimes have a high caloric content.

canela *n, f* • kanela   **cinnamon**

¿Por qué no añades un poco de canela? ► Why don't you add a little cinnamon?

cantidad *n, f* • kantiðað   **amount / quantity**

Estamos importando una gran cantidad de comestibles. ► We import a large quantity of food.

capacidad *n, f* • kapaθiðað, kapasiðað   **ability / capacity**

La capacidad de este ascensor es de diez personas. ► This elevator's capacity is ten people.

cáscara *n, f* • kAskara   **peel / rind / shell / skin**

Se resbaló con una cáscara de plátano. ► He slipped on a banana peel.

cazo *n, m* • kaθo, kaso   **pot**

¿Es un <u>cazo</u> nuevo? ▸ Is this a new <u>pot</u>?

cerveza *n, f* • θerβeθa, serβesa **beer**

Las botellas de <u>cerveza</u> están hechas de vidrio. ▸ <u>Beer</u> bottles are made of glass.

cítricos *n, m* • θItrikos, sItrikos **citrus fruits / plants**

Suelo comer muchos <u>cítricos</u>. ▸ I usually <u>eat</u> a lot of citrus fruits.

cocer *v* • koθer, koser **to boil / to bake**

¿Podrías <u>cocer</u> estos huevos? ▸ Could you <u>boil</u> these eggs?

cocinar *v* • koθinar, kosinar **to cook**

A él le gusta <u>cocinar</u> para su familia. ▸ He likes to <u>cook</u> for his family.

colorantes *n, m* • kolorantes **coloring**

Este producto no tiene <u>colorantes</u>. ▸ This product has not <u>colorings</u>.

comida *n, f* • komiδa **food / lunch / meal**

La <u>comida</u> de aquí no es muy buena. ▸ The <u>food</u> isn't very good here.

completo/a *adj* • kompleto **complete**

¿Está <u>completo</u> este juego de té? ▸ Is this tea set <u>complete</u>?

composición *n, f* • komposiθjOn, komposisjOn **composition**

Calentar el agua no cambia su <u>composición</u> química. ▸ Heating water does not change its chemical composition.

compuesto *n, m* • kompwesto   **compound / composed**

El curry en polvo está compuesto por varias especias. ▸ Curry powder is composed of several spices.

condimentar *v* • kondimentaɾ   **to season**

¿Cómo condimentas tu comida? ▸ How do you season your food?

congelador *n, m* • koŋxelaðoɾ   **freezer**

Voy a poner el helado en el congelador. ▸ I'm putting the ice cream in the freezer.

congelar *v* • koŋxelaɾ   **to freeze**

Las bayas se pueden congelar. ▸ Berries can be frozen.

conserva *n, f* • konserβa   **canned / tinned food**

Me gustan las frutas en conserva. ▸ I like canned fruits.

conservantes *n, m* • konserβantes   **preservatives**

A mí me gusta el yogur sin conservantes. ▸ I like the yogurt without preservatives.

conservar *v* • konserβaɾ   **to keep / to preserve**

Si quieres conservar carne por harto tiempo, congélala. ▸ If you want to keep meat for long, freeze it.

consumir *v* • konsumiɾ   **to consume / eat / drink**

Prefiero el azúcar sin refinar antes que <u>consumir</u> edulcorantes. ► I prefer unrefined sugar rather than <u>consuming</u> sweeteners.

cortar *v* • koɾtaɾ   **to cut / to chop**

Este cuchillo no va a <u>cortar</u> bien. ► This knife won't <u>cut</u> well.

crudo/a *adj* • kɾuðo   **rare / raw**

No come pescado <u>crudo</u>. ► He doesn't eat <u>raw</u> fish.

cualidad *n, f* • kwaliðað   **property / quality**

Mejoramos la <u>cualidad</u>. ► We improved the <u>quality</u>.

cubiertos *n, m* • kuβjeɾtos   **cutlery**

¿Necesitamos más <u>cubiertos</u>? ► Do we need more <u>cutlery</u>?

cubrir *v* • kuβɾiɾ   **to cover**

Ese dinero es suficiente para <u>cubrir</u> los gastos. ► That's enoygh money to <u>cover</u> the expenses.

cucharada *n, f* • kuʧaɾaða   **spoonful / tablespoon**

Siempre le hecho una <u>cucharada</u> de miel a mi té. ► I always add a <u>spoonful</u> of honey to my tea.

delgado/a *adj* • delgaðo   **thin / slim**

¿Estás más <u>delgado</u>? ► Are you <u>thinner</u>?

demasiado *adv* • demasjaðo   **too much**

Comer <u>demasiado</u> no es bueno para el cuerpo. ► Eating <u>too much</u> is bad for the health.

desarrollar _v_ • desaro/ar — **to develop / to build up**

Él ha estado haciendo ejercicio para desarrollar sus músculos. ▸ He has been working out to develop his muscles.

descongelar _v_ • deskoŋxelar — **to defrost**

Debo descongelar el pescado ahora. ▸ I should defrost the fish right now.

desnutrido/a _adj_ • deznutriðo — **malnourished / undernourished**

El médico dijo que el niño estaba desnutrido. ▸ The doctor said the boy was undernourished.

dieta equilibrada _n, f_ • djeta ekiliβraða — **balanced diet**

¿Tienes una dieta equilibrada? ▸ Do you have a balanced diet?

digerir _v_ • dixerir — **to digest**

Mastica bien tu comida para que se pueda digerir bien. ▸ Chew your food well so it can be digested properly.

digestión _n, f_ • dixestjOn — **digestion**

Cuanto más cocida esté la carne, más rápida será la digestión. ▸ The better cooked the meat is, the quicker its digestion.

digestivo/a _adj_ • dixestiβo — **digestive**

Es un problema del aparato digestivo. ▸ This is a problem of the digestive system.

dulce _n, m_ • dulθe, dulse — **candy / sweet**

Quiero algo dulce. ▸ I want something sweet.

edulcorante *n, m* • eðulkorante   **sweetener**

La stevia es utilizada como edulcorante. ▸ Stevia is used as a sweetener.

eliminar *v* • eliminar   **to eliminate / to remove**

Abrí las ventanas para eliminar la humedad de la pieza. ▸ I opened the windows to remove the damp from the room.

embutido *n, m* • embutiðo   **cold meat**

¿Cuál es tu embutido favorito? ▸ What's your favorite cold meat?

empalagoso/a *adj* • empalayoso   **overly sweet / oversweet**

Este postre es empalagoso para mí. ▸ I find this dessert oversweet.

enfriar *v* • emfrjar   **to cool / to chill**

Es mejor enfriar el vino blanco antes de servirlo. ▸ It's better to chill white wine before you serve it.

engordar *v* • eŋgorðar   **to put on weight**

He engordado mucho. ▸ I've put on so much weight.

entrante *n, m* • entrante   **starter**

Vamos a servir los entrantes. ▸ Let's serve the starters.

escurrir *v* • eskurir   **to drain**

¿Por qué escurres la verdura? ‣ Why do you drain the vegetables?

especias *n, f* • espeθjas, espesjas **spices**

El curry en polvo está compuesto por varias especias. ‣ Curry powder is composed of several spices.

espinacas *n, f* • espinakas **spinach**

Ella le obligó a comer espinacas. ‣ She forced him to eat spinach.

espumadera *n, f* • espumaðera **slotted spoon / skimmer**

Saqué la espuma de la sopa hirviendo con una espumadera. ‣ I skimmed the simmering soup with a skimmer.

evitar *v* • eβitar **evitar**

Evitamos ciertos productos. ‣ We avoid certain products.

excesivo/a *adj* • eksθesiβo, ekssesiβo **excessive**

¿No es eso excesivo? ‣ Isn't that excessive?

exceso *n, m* • eksθeso, eksseso **excess / extra**

Todo exceso es abominable. ‣ All excess is abominable.

fibra *n, f* • fiβra **fibre**

Necesitas comer más fibra. ‣ You need to eat more fibre.

freír *v* • freIr **to fry**

Voy a freír estos huevos. ▸ I'm going to fry these eggs.

frito/a *adj* • frito   **fried**

Comí arroz frito y bebí algo de cerveza. ▸ I ate fried rice and drank some beer.

frugal *adj* • fruɣal   **frugal / light**

Prefiero una dieta frugal. ▸ I prefer a light diet.

frutería *n, f* • fruteɾía   **fruit shop / greengrocer's**

¿Hay alguna frutería cerca? ▸ Is there a fruit shop near?

fuego *n, m* • fweɣo   **fire / light**

Ellos se sentaron al lado del fuego. ▸ They sat down by the fire.

gamba *n, f* • gamba   **prawn / shrimp**

Odio las gambas. ▸ I hate prawns.

garbanzos *n, m* • garβanθos, garβansos   **chickpeas**

El segundo plato lleva garbanzos, pollo, carne, chorizo y patatas. ▸ The second course has chickpeas, chicken, meat, sausage and potato.

gastronómico/a *adj* • gastronOmiko   **gastronomic**

Vamos a hacer una ruta gastronómica. ▸ We're going on a gastronomic tour.

hervir *v* • erβir   **to boil**

El agua se evapora después de hervir. ▸ Water will evaporate after it is boiled.

43

hornear *v* • ornear   **to bake**

En primavera del año pasado fui a clases de cocina y aprendí a <u>hornear</u> pan.
▸ I took a cooking class last spring and learned to <u>bake</u> bread.

hornilla *n, f* • orniʎa   **burner / hob**

Esta <u>hornilla</u> no funciona. ▸ This <u>burner</u> doesn't work.

horno *n, m* • orno   **oven**

¡Este olor podría provenir del <u>horno</u>! ▸ This smell might come from the <u>oven</u>!

indigesto/a *adj* • indixesto   **hard to digest**

Algunas frutas son <u>indigestas</u>. ▸ Some fruits are hard to <u>digest</u>.

ingerir *v* • iŋxerir   **to ingest / consume**

¿Ha <u>ingerido</u> usted algún alimento raro? ▸ Have you <u>consumed</u> any strange food?

insípido/a *adj* • insɪpiðo   **tasteless**

Esto está <u>insípido</u>. ▸ This is <u>tasteless</u>.

integral *adj* • inteɣral   **wholegrain**

Los expertos en nutrición modernos ponen énfasis en comer pan <u>integral</u> y más verduras. ▸ Modern healthy eating experts put emphasis on eating <u>wholemeal</u> bread and eating more vegetables.

lácteo/a *adj* • lAkteo   **dairy**

¿Comes productos lácteos? ▸ Do you eat dairy products?

licor *n, m* • likoɾ — **liqueur / liquor**

En este negocio no se vende licor. ▸ Liquor is not sold at this store.

ligero/a *adj* • lixeɾo — **light / soft**

Normalmente tomo un desayuno ligero. ▸ I usually have a light breakfast.

líquido/a *adj* • llkiðo — **liquid**

El agua es un líquido. Cuando se congela, se vuelve sólido. ▸ Water is liquid. When it freezes, it becomes solid.

lleno/a *adj* • ʎeno — **full**

Estoy lleno. ▸ I'm full.

madurar *v* • maðuɾaɾ — **to ripen**

¿Cómo puedo madurar esta fruta más rápido? ▸ How can I ripen this fruit faster?

maduro/a *adj* • maðuɾo — **mature / ripe**

Este limón no está maduro. ▸ This lemon isn't ripe.

mantequilla *n, f* • mantekiʎa — **butter**

La leche se procesa para hacer mantequilla o queso. ▸ Milk is made into butter and cheese.

medida *n, f* • meðiða — **measure / part**

La caloría es una medida exacta de la energía en los alimentos. ▸ The calorie is an exact measure of the energy in food.

menú *n, m* • menU   **menu**

Aquí está su menú. ‣ Here is your menu.

merendar *v* • merendar   **to have a snack**

Para merendar, ella come frutas o nueces. ‣ For snacks, she eats fruit or nuts.

mezcla *n, f* • meθkla, meskla   **blend / mix / mixture**

¿Cuántos moles del compuesto químico hay en esta mezcla? ‣ How many moles of the compound are in this mixture?

mezclar *v* • meθklar, mesklar   **to blend / to mix**

No se puede mezclar aceite con agua. ‣ You can't mix oil with water.

mora *n, f* • mora   **blackberry**

¿Os gusta la mermelada de mora? ‣ Do you like blackberry jam?

nata *n, f* • nata   **cream**

Un café con azúcar y nata, por favor. ‣ Coffee, please, with cream and sugar.

néctar *n, m* • nEktar   **nectar**

¿Cuál es la diferencia entre el néctar y el zumo? ‣ What's the difference between nectar and juice?

nutrición *n, f* • nutriθjOn, nutrisjOn   **nutrition**

La buena nutrición también es una ciencia, y como tal, se puede aprender.
▸ Good nutrition is also a science and, as such, can be learnt.

nutricionista *n, f/m* • nutriθjonista, nutrisjonista   **nutritionist**

¿Qué te dijo la nutricionista sobre tu dieta? ▸ What did the nutritionist tell
you about your diet?

nutritivo/a *adj* • nutritiβo   **nutritious / nourishing**

Tomé un desayuno nutritivo. ▸ I ate a nutritious breakfast.

obesidad *n, f* • oβesiðað   **obesity**

Un estudio ha probado que comer demasiado rápido incrementa tus posibilidades de sufrir obesidad. ▸ A study has proved that eating too fast in-
creases your chance of obesity.

obeso/a *adj* • oβeso   **obese**

La doctora me dijo que estoy obeso. ▸ The doctor told me I am obese.

olla *n, f* • oʎa   **pan / pot**

No había mucho azúcar en la olla. ▸ There wasn't much sugar in the pot.

olor *n, m* • oloɾ   **odour / scent / smell**

El olor a comida me dio hambre. ▸ The smell of food made me hungry.

orgánico/a *adj* • orɣAniko   **organic**

El ácido salicílico es un compuesto orgánico. ▸ Salicylic acid is an organic
compound.

pastel *n, m* • pastel   **cake / pie**

47

Corta el pastel con ese cuchillo. ► Cut the cake with that knife.

pastelería *n, f* • pastelerIa   **cake shop / patisserie**

Hay una pastelería cerca de mi casa. ► There's a patisserie near my house.

pesado/a *adj* • pesaðo   **heavy**

¿Cuál de los dos es el más pesado? ► Which is the heavier of the two?

picante *adj* • pikante   **hot / spicy**

No me gusta la comida picante. ► I don't like spicy food.

picar *v* • pikaɾ   **to get a bite / to snack**

¿Tenemos algo para picar? ► Do we have anything I can snack on?

pimienta *n, f* • pimjenta   **pepper**

¿Quieres que se le ponga pimienta? ► Do you want pepper on it?

pizca *n, f* • piθka, piska   **pinch**

Ahora vamos a echarle una pizca de sal. ► No we're going to add a pinch of salt.

porción *n, f* • poɾθjOn, poɾsjOn   **portion / piece**

¿Desea una porción entera o media porción? ► Would you like a whole or half portion?

postre *n, m* • postre   **dessert**

¿Qué quieres de <u>postre</u>? ▸ What would you like for <u>dessert</u>?

precio *n, m* • preθjo, presjo **price**

El <u>precio</u> de las verduras cambia de un día a otro. ▸ The <u>price</u> of vegetables varies from day to day.

precocinado/a *adj* • prekoθinaðo, prekosinaðo **pre-cooked**

Nunca compro comida <u>precocinada</u>. ▸ I never buy <u>pre-cooked</u> food.

preparación *n, f* • preparaθjOn, preparasjOn **preparation**

La <u>preparación</u> comienza mañana. ▸ The <u>preparation</u> starts tomorrow

preparado/a *adj* • preparaðo **prepared / ready**

¿Está <u>preparado</u> el desayuno? ▸ Is breakfast <u>ready</u>?

preparar *v* • preparar **to prepare**

Todas las mañanas ayuda a su madre a <u>preparar</u> el desayuno en la cocina. ▸ Every morning she helps her mother to <u>prepare</u> breakfast in the kitchen.

prevenir *v* • preβenir **to prevent**

¿Somos capaces de <u>prevenir</u> la enfermedad? ▸ Are we able to <u>prevent</u> disease?

probar *v* • proβar **to taste / to try**

Hay algo que quiero <u>probar</u>. ▸ There's something I want to <u>try</u>.

ración *n, f* • raθjOn, rasjOn **helping / portion**

La tarta de manzana de su tía era deliciosa, así que se sirvió otra <u>ración</u>. ▸

His aunt's apple pie was delicious, so he had a second helping.

rallar *v* • raʎar **to grate**

¿Rallaste el queso? ▸ Did you grate the cheese?

rebozar *v* • reβoθar, reβosar **to batter**

Primero hay que rebozarlo en harina. ▸ First you have to batter it in flour.

receta *n, f* • reθeta, reseta **prescription / recipe**

¿Me darías la receta para tu ensalada? ▸ Would you give me the recipe for your salad?

recomendable *adj* • rekomendaβle **advisable**

Es recomendable beber más agua. ▸ It is advisable to drink more water.

régimen *n, m* • rEximen **diet / regime**

Estoy a régimen. ▸ I'm on a diet.

remover *v* • remoβer **to stir**

Remueva la sopa unos segundos. ▸ Stir the soup for a few seconds.

retirar *v* • retirar **to take back / to clear**

¿Me ayudas a retirar los platos? ▸ Can you help me clear the table?

sabor *n, m* • saβor **flavor / taste**

El ajo se usa para mejorar el sabor de las comidas. ▸ Garlic is used to improve the taste of food.

sabroso/a *adj* • saβroso

delicious / tasteful

Mi padre me cocinará un desayuno sabroso mañana por la mañana. ▸ My father will cook me a delicious meal tomorrow morning.

salsa *n, f* • salsa

dip / dressing / sauce

La compañía produce salsa de soya y otros productos alimenticios. ▸ The company produces soy sauce and other food products.

sartén *n, f* • saɾtEn

frying pan

¿Tienes una sartén más grande? ▸ Do you have a bigger frying pan?

sazonar *v* • saθonaɾ, sasonaɾ

to season

La sal se usa para sazonar la comida. ▸ Salt is used to season food.

sobrante *adj* • soβɾante

leftovers

¿Qué hacemos con la comida sobrante? ▸ What can we do with the leftovers?

sobrepeso *n, m* • soβɾepeso

overweight

Se considera que una persona con un IMC de 25 a 29 padece sobrepeso. ▸ A person with a BMI of 25 to 29 is considered overweight.

tapa *n, f* • tapa

appetizer / cover / lid / top

¿Dónde está la tapa de la sartén? ▸ Where's the pan lid?

tarta *n, f* • taɾta

cake / pie / tart

Ella está comprando una tarta en la panadería. ▸ She is buying a cake in the bakery.

té *n, m* • tE   **tea**

¿Quisieras café o té? ▸ Would you like coffee or tea?

temperatura *n, f* • temperatura   **temperature**

A bajas temperaturas, el agua se convierte en hielo. ▸ At low temperatures, water turns to ice.

tomar *v* • tomar   **to drink / to get / to have / to take**

Me gustaría tomar chocolate caliente. ▸ I'd like to have some hot chocolate.

torta *n, f* • torta   **cake / sandwich**

Esta torta es dulce. ▸ This cake is sweet.

tostar *v* • tostar   **to toast**

Voy a tostar el pan. ▸ I'm toasting the bread.

trocear *v* • troθear, trosear   **to chop**

¿Puedes trocear esta verdura? ▸ Will you chop these vegetables?

trozo *n, m* • troθo, troso   **part / piece**

Ella quería un trozo de tarta pero ya no quedaba más. ▸ She wanted a piece of cake, but there was none left.

untar *v* • untar   **to spread**

¿Quieres untar un poco de mantequilla? ▸ Would you like to spread a bit of butter?

vacío/a *adj* • baθIo, basIo   **empty**

Encontré el vaso vacío. ▸ I found the glass empty.

vainilla *n, f* • bainiʎa   **vanilla**

Dos helados de vainilla, por favor. ▸ Two vanilla ice creams, please.

vegano *n, f/m* • beɣano   **vegan**

¿Eres vegetariano o vegano? ▸ Are you vegetarian or vegan?

vegetariano *n, f/m* • bexetaɾjano   **vegetarian / veggie**

Soy vegetariano. ▸ I am a vegetarian.

vender *v* • bendeɾ   **to sell**

El arroz se vende por kilos. ▸ Rice is sold by the kilogram.

vitamina *n, f* • bitamina   **vitamin**

Esta dieta está repleta de vitaminas. ▸ This diet is full of vitamins.

vomitar *v* • bomitaɾ   **to vomit**

Me puse a vomitar. ▸ I started to vomit.

3

Personality & Behavior

abierto/a *adj* • aβjeɾto   **open-minded**

¿Me consideras una persona abierta? ▸ Do you consider me an open-minded person?

aburrido/a *adj* • aβuriðo   **bored / boring**

Para decirte la verdad, estoy completamente aburrido. ▸ To tell you the truth, I'm completely bored.

aconsejar *v* • akonsexaɾ   **to advise / give advice**

Voy a darte un consejo. ▸ I'm going to give you a piece of advice.

afectuoso/a *adj* • afektwoso   **affectionate**

Es una mujer muy afectuosa. ▸ She's a very affectionate woman.

agradable *adj* • aɣɾaðaβle   **kind / nice / friendly**

Es agradable estar en familia. ▸ It is nice to be among family.

aguafiestas *n, f/m* • aɣwafjestas   **spoilsport / killjoy**

Tom es muy aguafiestas. ▸ Tom is such a killjoy.

alegrar *v* • aleɣɾaɾ   **to cheer up / to make happy**

Tienes muchas razones para alegrarte. ▸ You have many reasons to cheer up.

alegre *adj* • aleɣɾe   **cheerful / happy / joyful**

Parece que está usted muy alegre hoy. ▸ It seems that you are very happy today.

alegría *n, f* • aleɣɾía   **cheer / happiness / joy**

Ni la alegría ni el dolor pueden durar para siempre. ▸ Neither joy nor sorrow can last forever.

amabilidad *n, f* • amaβiliðað   **courtesy / kindness**

Le agradezco mucho su amabilidad. ▸ I thank you very much for your kindness.

amable *adj* • amaβle   **gentle / kind / nice**

Sé amable con la gente mayor. ▸ Be kind to old people.

amante *adj/n* • amante   **loving / lover**

Me gustan los gatos tanto, no puedo evitarlo, soy un amante loco de los gatos. ▸ I love cats so much, I can't help it, I'm a crazy cat lover.

amigo/a *n, f/m* • amiɣo   **friend**

Fui al aeropuerto a despedir a un amigo. ▸ I went to the airport to see my friend off.

amistad *n, f* • amistað   **friendship**

Todos estamos unidos por la amistad. ▸ We're all linked in friendship.

amistoso/a *adj* • amistoso   **amicable / friendly**

Él es amistoso con todos sus compañeros. ▸ He's friendly with all his class-mates.

antipatía *n, f* • antipatIa   **dislike**

Sólo tengo antipatía hacia ella. ▸ I only feel dislike for her.

antipático/a *adj* • antipAtiko   **unfriendly**

No creo que sea antipático. ▸ I don't think he's unfriendly.

apasionado/a *adj* • apasjonaðo   **passionate**

Ella tenía un apasionado interés por la música. ▸ She had a passionate in-terest in music.

astucia *n, f* • astuθja, astusja   **cleverness / cunning**

Quiso presumir su astucia en la lección, pero fracasó. ▸ She wanted to show off her cleverness during class, but she failed.

astuto/a *adj* • astuto   **clever / cunning / sly**

Él no es sabio sino astuto. ▸ He is not wise but clever.

atreverse *v* • atreßerse   **to dare**

¡Cómo te atreves! ▸ How dare you!

atrevido/a *adj* • atreβiðo   **daring**

Eres bastante atrevido. ▸ You're quite daring.

autoestima *n, f* • autoestima   **self-esteem**

Ella adora leer frases de autoestima. ▸ She loves reading sentences about self-esteem.

cabezota *adj* • kaβeθota, kaβesota   **stubborn**

Es una cabezota. ▸ She's a stubborn girl.

callado/a *adj* • kaʎaðo   **quiet**

Has estado muy callada. ▸ You've been very quiet.

calma *n, f* • kalma   **calm / quiet**

Todo está en calma. ▸ All is quiet.

capaz *adj* • kapaθ, kapas   **able / capable**

En esta compañía, debes ser capaz de hablar inglés o español. ▸ You must be able to speak either English or Spanish in this company.

chivato *n, f/m* • ʧiβato   **informer / rat / snitch**

¡Es un chivato! ▸ He's a snitch!

cobarde *adj* • koβarðe   **coward**

Él no es más que un cobarde. ▸ He is nothing more than a coward.

cobardía *n, f* • koβarðIa   **cowardice**

En nuestras vidas, tenemos tres o cuatro ocasiones de mostrar valentía, pero todos los días, tenemos la ocasión de mostrar la falta de cobardía. ▸ In our lives, we have three or four occasions of showing bravery, but every day, we have the occasion to show a lack of cowardice.

complicado/a *adj* • komplikaðo   **complex / complicated**

Lo que a ti te parece simple, a mí me parece complicado. ▸ What seems simple to you seems complex to me.

comportamiento *n, m* • komportamjento   **behavior**

No puedo soportar más su comportamiento. ▸ I can't stand his behavior anymore.

comprensivo/a *adj* • komprensiβo   **sympathetic / understanding**

Él es muy comprensivo. ▸ He's very understanding.

confianza *n, f* • komfjanθa, komfjansa   **trust**

Perdí mi confianza en él. ▸ I lost my trust in him.

conflicto *n, m* • komflikto   **conflict**

Tenemos que evitar un conflicto en la medida posible. ▸ We have to avoid a conflict as far as possible.

cordial *adj* • korðjal   **friendly / hearty**

Manteniendo una charla con él, lo encontré inquieto pero cordial. ▸ On having a talk with him, I found him troubled but <u>friendly</u>.

cordialidad *n, f* • korðjaliðað **friendliness / warmth**

La <u>cordialidad</u> es una bonita virtud. ▸ <u>Friendliness</u> is a nice virtue.

decaído/a *adj* • dekaĭðo **low / blue**

¿Por qué estás tan <u>decaída</u>? ▸ Why are you feeling so <u>blue</u>?

desagradable *adj* • desaɣraðaβle **unfriendly / unpleasant**

Él tiene una mirada <u>desagradable</u>. ▸ He has an <u>unpleasant</u> look in his eyes.

desconfiado/a *adj* • deskomfjaðo **distrustful / suspicious**

Tal vez yo no debería ser tan <u>desconfiado</u>. ▸ Maybe I shouldn't be so <u>suspicious</u>.

desconfianza *n, f* • deskomfjanθa, deskomfjansa **distrust / mistrust**

La <u>desconfianza</u> es la madre de la seguridad. ▸ <u>Mistrust</u> is the mother of safety.

desorganizado/a *adj* • desorɣaniθaðo, desorɣanisaðo **disorganized / messy / untidy**

¿De verdad piensas que soy <u>desorganizada</u>? ▸ Do you really think I am <u>disorganized</u>?

despreciable *adj* • despreθjaβle, despresjaβle **despicable**

Nada es más <u>despreciable</u> que respeto fundado en el miedo. ▸ Nothing is more despicable than respect based on fear.

disciplinado/a adj • disθiplinaðo, dissiplinaðo
well-behaved

disciplined /

No es lo suficientemente disciplinado. ‣ He's not disciplined enough.

divertido/a adj • diβertiðo

amusing / fun / funny

Jugar fuera es muy divertido. ‣ It's a lot of fun playing outdoors.

divorciarse v • diβorθjarse, diβorsjarse

to divorce

¿Por qué se divorciaron? ‣ Why did they divorce?

egoísta adj • eɣoIsta

selfish

Quizás tengas razón, fui un egoísta. ‣ Perhaps you are right, I have been selfish.

enamorado/a adj • enamoraðo

in love

Estoy enamorado de ella. ‣ I'm in love with her.

enemigo/a n, f/m • enemiɣo

enemy

Derrotamos al enemigo. ‣ We defeated the enemy.

enfadado/a adj • emfaðaðo

angry / cross / mad / upset

Él está enfadado todavía. ‣ He is still angry.

enfadar v • emfaðar

to get angry

Me hizo enfadar tanto en el teléfono que le colgué. ‣ She made me so angry on the telephone that I hung up on her.

enfado *n, m* • emfaðo **anger**

Tal era su enfado que perdió el control. ▸ His anger was such that he lost control of himself.

engañar *v* • eŋgaɲar **to cheat / to deceive**

Él sabe muy bien cómo engañar a la gente. ▸ He knows very well how to deceive people.

entristecer *v* • entristeθer, entristeser **to sadden**

La noticia nos entristeció. ▸ The news saddened us.

entusiasmado/a *adj* • entusjazmaðo **eager / enthusiastic / excited**

Ocultó sus sentimientos y fingió estar entusiasmado. ▸ He hid his emotions and pretended to be enthusiastic.

esperanza *n, f* • esperanθa, esperansa **hope**

No hay que perder la esperanza. ▸ Don't give up hope.

estado *n, m* • estaðo **state / status**

¿Por qué estaba en ese estado? ▸ Why was she in such a state?

estereotipo *n, m* • estereotipo **stereotype**

Es un viejo estereotipo. ▸ It's an old stereotype.

estima *n, f* • estima **esteem**

Tengo una gran estima por ti. ▸ I have a great esteem for you.

estimar *v* • estimar **to appreciate / to value**

Por supuesto que estimo a mis amigos. ▸ Of course I appreciate my friends.

estresado/a *adj* • estresaðo **stressed out**

Siempre estoy estresado. ▸ I'm always stressed out.

estresante *adj* • estresante **stressful**

Es una situación estresante. ▸ This is a stressful situation.

extraño/a *adj* • ekstraɲo **bizarre / odd / strange**

Es extraño que nadie nos conozca. ▸ It's strange that nobody knows us.

extrovertido/a *adj* • ekstroβertiðo **extroverted / outgoing**

Eres extrovertido. ▸ You're extroverted.

familiar *adj* • familjar **familiar / family / relative**

Los turnos de trabajo pueden ser sumamente perjudiciales para la vida familiar. ▸ Working shifts can be extremely disruptive to family life.

festivo/a *adj* • festiβo **festive / merry / holiday**

Hoy estamos de un humor festivo. ▸ Today we are in a merry mood.

firme *adj* • firme **adamant / firm**

Él tiene un <u>firme</u> propósito en la vida. ▸ He has a <u>firm</u> purpose in life.

formal *adj* • formal   **formal**

No tienes que ser tan <u>formal</u>. ▸ You don't have to be so <u>formal</u>.

fragilidad *n, f* • fraxiliðað   **fragility / frailty**

Su <u>fragilidad</u> es evidente. ▸ His <u>frailty</u> is obvious.

fuerza *n, f* • fwerθa, fwersa   **strength**

He subestimado la <u>fuerza</u> de mi adversario. ▸ I have underestimated the <u>strength</u> of my opponent.

gana *n, f* • gana   **desire / wish**

No tenía ninguna <u>gana</u> de hacerlo. ▸ I didn't have any <u>desire</u> to do that.

generoso/a *adj* • xeneroso   **generous**

Sea usted <u>generoso</u>, no piense solamente en sus defectos. ▸ Be <u>generous</u>; don't think only of his faults.

harto/a *adj* • arto   **fed up / tired**

Estoy <u>harto</u> de todas sus mentiras. ▸ I'm <u>fed up</u> with all their lies.

hipócrita *adj* • ipOkrita   **hypocrite**

No seas <u>hipócrita</u>. ▸ Don't be a <u>hypocrite</u>.

honrado/a *adj* • onraðo   **honest**

Pensé que era una mujer <u>honrada</u>, pero me equivoqué. ▸ I thought she was an honest woman, But I was wrong.

humano/a *adj* • umana   **human / humane**

En las profundidades del alma humana se ocultan oscuros sentimientos. ▸
In the depths of human soul, dark feelings lurk.

impaciencia *n, f* • impaθjenθja, impasjensja   **impatience**

La impaciencia no es buena. ▸ Impatience is no good.

impaciente *adj* • impaθjente, impasjente   **eager / impatient**

No deberías ser impaciente con los niños. ▸ You shouldn't be impatient with
children.

impersonal *adj* • impersonal   **impersonal**

Sentí su trato frío e impersonal. ▸ I felt his cold and impersonal treatment.

incapaz *adj* • iŋkapaθ, iŋkapas   **helpless / unable**

Él es incapaz de hacer eso. ▸ He is unable to do it.

indignado/a *adj* • indiɣnaðo   **angry / outraged**

¡Estamos indignados! ▸ We are outraged!

inestable *adj* • inestaβle   **unstable**

¿Por qué es tan inestable? ▸ Why is he so unstable?

informal *adj* • imformal   **casual / informal**

Este es un acuerdo informal. ▸ This is an informal agreement.

informalidad *n, f* • imformaliðað   **informality / unreliability**

Disfruté de la informalidad de la fiesta. ▸ I enjoyed the informality of the party.

injusto/a *adj* • iŋxusto   **unfair**

Sería injusto si lo tratáramos tan mal. ▸ It would be unfair if we treated him so badly.

inmadurez *n, f* • immaðureθ, immaðures   **immaturity**

Su inmadurez me molesta. ▸ Her immaturity annoys me.

inseguridad *n, f* • inseɣuriðað   **insecurity**

La adolescencia es usualmente un periodo de inseguridad. ▸ Adolescence is often a period of insecurity.

inseguro/a *adj* • inseɣuro   **hesitant / insecure**

Tras el terremoto, el vecindario se sentía inseguro. ▸ After the earthquake the neighbourhood felt insecure.

insensible *adj* • insensiβle   **insensitive**

No quiero parecer insensible. ▸ I don't want to seem insensitive.

interacción *n, f* • interakθjOn, interaksjOn   **interaction**

La interacción social es el fundamento mismo de la vida social. ▸ Social interaction is the very foundation of social life.

intimidad *n, f* • intimiðað   **familiarity / intimacy / privacy**

La intimidad es esencial en mi vida. ▸ Privacy is essential in my life.

íntimo/a *adj* • Intimo   **close / intimate**

Es una amiga íntima. ▸ She's a close friend.

irracional *adj* • iraθjonal, irasjonal   **irrational**

Él es estúpido e irracional. ▸ He's stupid and irrational.

irresponsable *adj* • iresponsaβle   **careless / irresponsible**

No puedes contar con ella porque es demasiado irresponsable. ▸ You cannot count on her because she's too irresponsible.

justo/a *adj* • xusto   **fair**

Eso no es justo. ▸ That's not fair.

leal *adj* • leal   **faithful / loyal / staunch**

Él es leal a su jefe. ▸ He is loyal to his boss.

lealtad *n, f* • lealtað   **allegiance / faithfulness / loyalty**

Yo exijo absoluta lealtad de todos mis empleados. ▸ I require absolute loyalty from all my employees.

madurez *n, f* • maðureθ, maðures   **maturity**

La buena disposición a tomar responsabilidad es una señal de madurez. ▸ Willingness to take responsibility is a sign of maturity.

mentalidad *n, f* • mentaliðað   **mentality / mindset / wit**

Todo cambia muy rápidamente y eso exige una nueva mentalidad entre los empleados de hoy. ▸ Everything changes very quickly, which calls for a new mindset among today's employees.

mentiroso/a adj • mentiroso   **liar**

Él es de todo menos mentiroso. ▸ He is anything but a liar.

molesto/a adj • molesto   **irritated / annoyed**

Estaba yo muy molesto con él. ▸ I was very much annoyed with him.

monótono/a adj • monOtono   **monotone / monotonous**

El paisaje era plano y monótono. ▸ The landscape was flat and monotonous.

natural adj • natural   **natural**

Supongamos que es natural. ▸ We assume that it is natural.

negatividad n, f • neɣatiβiðað   **negativity**

No soporto tu negatividad. ▸ I can't stand your negativity.

nervioso/a adj • nerβjoso   **nervous / anxious**

El zumbido de las abejas me pone un poco nerviosa. ▸ The buzzing of the bees makes me a little nervous.

obedecer v • oβeðeθer, oβeðeser   **to obey**

Deberíamos obedecer la ley. ▸ We should obey the law.

obediente adj • oβeðjente   **obedient**

La niña pequeá no era obediente. ▸ The little girl wasn't obedient.

odiar v • oðjaɾ   **to hate**

Estoy empezando a odiar este pueblo. ▸ I'm really starting to hate this town.

odio n, m • oðjo   **hatred**

Ella sentía algo entre el amor y el odio. ▸ She felt something between love and hatred.

ofendido/a adj • ofendiðo   **offended / humiliated**

Tu acto ha ofendido su dignidad. ▸ Your action has offended his dignity.

optimista adj • optimista   **optimist / optimistic / upbeat**

Él es bastante optimista. ▸ He is rather optimistic.

ordinario/a adj • oɾðinaɾjo   **ordinary / vulgar**

No hice nada fuera de lo ordinario. ▸ I did nothing out of the ordinary.

organizado/a adj • oɾɣaniθaðo, oɾɣanisaðo   **organized**

No soy muy organizado. ▸ I'm not very organized.

osado/a adj • osaðo   **daring / plucky**

No soy lo suficientemente osada. ▸ I'm not daring enough.

osar v • osaɾ   **to dare**

No osé saltar. ▸ I didn't dare to jump.

pacificar *v* • paθifikaɾ, pasifikaɾ   **to pacify**

Fue imposible pacificar la zona. ▸ It was impossible to pacify the area.

pacífico/a *adj* • paθIfiko, pasIfiko   **orderly / peaceful / quiet**

Creo en un mundo pacífico. ▸ I believe in a peaceful world.

paz *n, f* • paθ, pas   **peace**

Él vive en paz. ▸ He lives in peace.

pereza *n, f* • peɾeθa, peɾesa   **laziness**

La victoria no emana de la pereza. ▸ Success does not come from laziness.

perezoso/a *adj* • peɾeθoso, peɾesoso   **lazy**

Fue regañado por su profesor por ser perezoso. ▸ He was scolded by his teacher for being lazy.

perfeccionismo *n, m* • peɾfekθjonizmo, peɾfeksjonizmo   **perfectionism**

Tu perfeccionismo es estresante. ▸ Your perfectionism is stressful.

perfeccionista *adj* • peɾfekθjonista, peɾfeksjonista   **perfectionist**

Mis amigos me odian por ser un perfeccionista. ▸ My friends hate me for being a perfectionist.

persistente *adj* • peɾsistente   **nagging / persistent**

Sé paciente y persistente. Estas cosas llevan tiempo. ▸ Be patient and persistent. These things take time.

personalidad *n, f* • personaliðað **personality**

Él tiene una personalidad maravillosa. ► He has a wonderful personality.

perverso/a *adj* • perβerso **evil**

Ese dictador era perverso. ► That dictator was evil.

pesimista *adj* • pesimista **pessimist / pessimistic**

Siempre es mejor ser optimista que pesimista. ► It is always better to be optimistic than pessimistic.

piedad *n, f* • pjeðað **clemency / mercy / piety / pity**

¡Tened piedad de mí! ► Have mercy on me!

posición *n, f* • posiθjOn, posisjOn **position**

Me explicó su posición. ► He explained his position to me.

positividad *n, f* • positiβiðað **positivity**

Necesito más positividad a mi alrededor. ► I need more positivity around me.

preocupado/a *adj* • preokupaðo **worried**

Estamos preocupados por su inesperada partida. ► We are worried because of his unexpected departure.

proceso *n, m* • proθeso, proseso **process**

La educación no debe limitarse a nuestra juventud, debe ser un proceso continuo a través de toda nuestra vida. ▸ Education must not be limited to our youth, but it must be a continuing process through our entire lives.

profundamente adv • profundamente **deeply**

Los acontecimientos recientes le han afectado profundamente. ▸ The recent events have affected him deeply.

profundidad n, f • profundiðað **depth / profundity**

Eso muestra la profundidad de su amor por su familia. ▸ It shows the depth of his love for his family.

raro/a adj • raɾo **bizarre / odd / peculiar / strange**

A veces él puede ser un chico raro. ▸ Sometimes he can be a strange guy.

razonable adj • raθonaβle, rasonaβle **reasonable / sensible**

¿Tienes alguna explicación razonable al respecto? ▸ Do you have any reasonable explanation about it?

razonar v • raθonaɾ, rasonaɾ **to reason**

La madre intentó razonar con su hijo. ▸ The mother tried to reason with her son.

relajado/a adj • relaxaðo **relaxed**

La gente de aquí lleva una vida relajada. ▸ The locals around here really live at a relaxed pace.

reservado/a adj • reserβaðo **reserved**

No seas tan reservado. ▸ Don't be so reserved.

sensibilidad *n, f* ● sensiβiliðað   **sensitivity / sentience**

Estaba conmovida por su sensibilidad. ▸ I was touched by his sensitivity.

sentimental *adj* ● sentimental   **feeling / sentimental / emotional**

A veces me pongo sentimental. ▸ I get emotional sometimes.

sentimiento *n, m* ● sentimjento   **feeling / sentiment**

Pienso que no puedes entender ese sentimiento a menos que seas de la misma
generación. ▸ I think you can't understand that feeling unless you're from
the same generation.

seriedad *n, f* ● serjeðað   **earnest / seriousness / severity**

Luego comprendió la seriedad de su error. ▸ She soon realized the seriousness of her error.

servicial *adj* ● serβiθjal, serβisjal   **helpful**

Es una chica muy servicial. ▸ She's a very helpful girl.

simpatía *n, f* ● simpatIa   **liking / friendliness**

Me encanta vuestra simpatía. ▸ I love your friendliness.

sincero/a *adj* ● sinθeɾo, sinseɾo   **honest / sincere**

Ponemos énfasis en la importancia de ser sincero. ▸ We lay emphasis on the
importance of being sincere.

sociable *adj* ● soθjaβle, sosjaβle   **sociable**

¿Crees que soy sociable? ▸ Do you think I'm sociable?

soledad *n, f* • soleðað   **loneliness / solitude**

La peor soledad es no sentirte a gusto contigo mismo. ▸ The worst loneliness is to not be comfortable with yourself.

solitario/a *adj* • solitarjo   **lonely / solitary**

Esta ciudad es fría y solitaria sin ti. ▸ This city is cold and lonely without you.

sonriente *adj* • sonrjente   **smiley**

Ella es demasiado sonriente. ▸ She is too smiley.

temeroso/a *adj* • temeroso   **scared**

No seas tan temerosa ▸ Don't be so scared.

temor *n, m* • temor   **fear**

A menudo, el temor a un mal nos lleva a otro peor. ▸ Often the fear of one evil leads us into a worse.

temperamental *adj* • temperamental   **temperamental**

Eres temperamental. ▸ You're temperamental.

tenaz *adj* • tenaθ, tenas   **tenacious**

Ser tenaz te ayudará. ▸ Being tenacious will help you.

tendencia *n, f* • tendenθja, tendensja   **bias / tendency / trend**

Yo no me apego a ninguna tendencia política en particular. ▸ I don't adhere to any particular political tendency.

terco/a adj • teɾko   **opinionated / stubborn**

Yo estoy aquí porque soy igual de terco que usted. ▸ I'm here because I'm just as stubborn as you are.

tímido/a adj • tImiðo   **shy**

Ella no es tan tímida como era antes. ▸ She is not so shy as she used to be.

trabajador adj • tɾaβaxaðoɾ   **hardworking**

El pueblo chino es excepcionalmente trabajador. ▸ The Chinese people are exceptionally hardworking.

tranquilidad n, f • tɾaŋkiliðað   **serenity / tranquillity**

Calma y tranquilidad es lo único que necesito para trabajar bien. ▸ Calmness and tranquility are all I need to work well.

tranquilizar v • tɾaŋkiliθaɾ, tɾaŋkilisaɾ   **to calm down**

Tienes que tranquilizarte. ▸ You need to calm down.

tranquilo/a adj • tɾaŋkilo   **peaceful / quiet**

Pasamos un día tranquilo en el campo. ▸ We spent a quiet day in the country.

tratar v • tɾataɾ   **to deal with / to treat**

¿Por qué me tratas así? ▸ Why do you treat me like that?

trato n, m • tɾato   **treatment**

Recibió un trato muy duro. ▸ He received rough treatment.

triste *adj* • triste   **blue / sad**

La película era tan triste que todos lloraron. ▸ The movie was so sad that everybody cried.

tristeza *n, f* • tristeθa, tristesa   **bleakness / sadness / sorrow**

Ocultó su tristeza tras una sonrisa. ▸ He hid his sadness behind a smile.

único/a *adj* • Uniko   **unique / only**

El ser humano es el único animal que utiliza el fuego. ▸ Man is the only animal that uses fire.

vago/a *adj* • baγo   **lazy / vague**

Él no es vago, al contrario, pienso que trabaja duro. ▸ He's not lazy. On the contrary, I think he's a hard worker.

valentía *n, f* • balentIa   **courage**

Su valentía es digna de elogio. ▸ His bravery is worthy of praise.

valiente *adj* • baljente   **brave / courageous**

Eres muy valiente. ▸ You are very brave.

verdad *n, f* • berðað   **truth**

Sólo la verdad es bella. ▸ Nothing is beautiful but the truth.

vil *adj* • bil   **despicable / vile**

Detrás de su sonrisa, él oculta un corazón vil. ▸ He conceals a despicable heart behind his smile.

virtud *n, f* • biɾtuð   **virtue**

La justicia y la bondad son virtudes. ▸ Justice and kindness are virtues.

vulgar *adj* • bulgaɾ   **common / tasteless / vulgar**

Él no es más que un vulgar granuja. ▸ He's nothing more than a common thug.

4 Body & Health

acné *n, m* • aknE   **acne**

Esta es una buena crema para el acné. ▸ This is a good acne cream.

aconsejable *adj* • akonsexaβle   **advisable**

Siempre es aconsejable preguntar a un médico. ▸ It's always advisable to
ask a doctor.

aconsejar *v* • akonsexar   **to advise**

¿Qué te aconsejó la doctora? ▸ What did the doctor advise you?

actividad *n, f* • aktiβiðað   **activity**

¿Cuál es tu actividad de verano favorita? ▸ What's your favorite summer
activity?

adecuado/a *adj* • aðekwaðo   **adequate / proper**

¿Cuál es la forma adecuada de lavar las verduras? ▸ What's a proper way
to wash vegetables?

adelgazar *v* • aðelgaθar, aðelgasar   **to lose weight**

¡Debo adelgazar! ▸ I have to lose weight!

afeitar *v* • afeitar̞ **to shave**

Él se afeita cuatro veces por semana. ▸ He shaves four times a week.

ágil *adj* • Axil **agile**

¿Cómo puede ser tan ágil tu abuela? ▸ How can your grandma be so agile?

agotamiento *n, m* • aɣotamjento **exhaustion**

No puedo explicar mi agotamiento. ▸ I cannot explain my exhaustion.

alimentación *n, f* • alimentaθjOn, alimentasjOn **diet / food / feeding**

No creo que tengas una buena alimentación. ▸ I don't think you have a proper diet.

alteración *n, f* • alteraθjOn, alterasjOn **alteration / disorder**

Tengo una seria alteración del sueño. ▸ I have a serious sleep disorder.

análisis de orina *n, m* • anAlisis de orina **urine analysis**

¿Por qué necesitas un análisis de orina? ▸ Why do you need a urine analysis?

análisis de sangre *n, m* • anAlisis de saŋɡɾe **blood test**

¿Cuándo te hiciste el último análisis de sangre? ▸ When was your last blood test?

anormal *adj* • anormal **aberrant / abnormal**

Es anormal comer tanto. ▸ It is abnormal to eat so much.

antibióticos *n, m* • antiβjOtikos   **antibiotics**

Soy alérgica a los antibióticos. ▸ I'm allergic to antibiotics.

arrugar *v* • aruɣaɾ   **to wrinkle**

¿Por qué arrugaron el entrecejo? ▸ Why did they wrinkle their eyebrows?

articulación *n, f* • artikulaθjOn, artikulasjOn   **articulation / joint**

El codo es la articulación entre el brazo y el antebrazo. ▸ The elbow is the joint between the arm and forearm.

astigmatismo *n, m* • astiɣmatizmo   **astigmatism**

¿Desde cuándo padeces astigmatismo? ▸ Since when do you suffer from astigmatism?

atención *n, f* • atenθjOn, atensjOn   **attention / care**

Deberías prestarle atención a tu bienestar. ▸ You should pay attention to your well-being.

atención primaria *n, f* • atensjOn primarja   **primary healthcare**

¿Está usted satisfecha con la atención primaria de la región? ▸ Are you satisfied with the primary healthcare in the area?

barriga *n, f* • bariɣa   **belly / tummy**

Tengo dolor de barriga. ▸ I have a bellyache.

beneficioso/a *adj* • benefiθjoso, benefisjoso   **beneficial**

¿Hacer ejercicio cada día es beneficioso para la salud? ▸ Is doing exercise every day beneficial to your health?

botiquín *n, m* • botikIn **medicine cabinet / first-aid kit**

Tom buscó su botiquín de primeros auxilios, pero no lo pudo encontrar. ▸ Tom looked for his first-aid kit, but couldn't find it.

cadera *n, f* • kaðera **hip**

Me duele la cadera. ▸ My hip hurts.

calmante *n, m* • kalmante **painkiller**

Creo que necesito un calmante para el dolor. ▸ I believe I need a painkiller for the pain.

calórico/a *adj* • kalOriko **caloric**

Esta bebida tiene un alto contenido calórico. ▸ This beverage has a high caloric content.

caminar *v* • kaminar **to walk**

Es bueno para la salud caminar todos los días. ▸ It's good for your health to walk every day.

cana *n, f* • kana **grey hair / white hair**

Tiene muchas canas. ▸ He has a lot of grey hair.

cansancio *n, m* • kansanθjo, kansansjo **exhaustion / tiredness**

Tu cansancio es lógico después de tanto trabajo. ▸ Your exhaustion is logical after so much work.

cara *n, f* • kaɾa   **face**

Ella tenía una cara pensativa. ▸ She had a thoughtful look on her face.

cardiólogo *n, f/m* • kaɾðjOloɣo   **cardiologist**

Ella es cardióloga. ▸ She's a cardiologist.

centro de salud *n, m* • sentɾo de saluð   **health center**

Soy enfermera en este centro de salud. ▸ I'm a nurse in this health center.

chequeo *n, m* • ʧekeo   **check / checkup**

Les hicieron un chequeo médico. ▸ They went through a medical check-up

cintura *n, f* • θintuɾa, sintuɾa   **waist**

¿Cuál es tu medida de cintura? ▸ What is your waist size?

cirugía *n, f* • θiɾuxIa, siɾuxIa   **surgery**

¿Necesito cirugía? ▸ Do I need surgery?

cirujano *n, f/m* • θiɾuxano, siɾuxano   **surgeon**

Mi padre es un cirujano experto. ▸ My father is an expert surgeon.

cita médica *n, f* • sita mEðika   **doctor's appointment**

¿Cuándo es tu cita médica? ▸ When's your doctor's appointment?

consciente *adj* • konsθjente, konssjente   **aware / conscious**

Él no fue consciente de su propio error. ▸ He was not conscious of his own mistake.

consejo *n, m* • konsexo **advice / tip**

Deja que te dé un consejo. ▸ Let me give you a piece of advice.

constipado/a *adj* • konstipaðo **to have a cold**

Estoy constipado. ▸ I've got a cold.

contracción *n, f* • kontrakθjOn, kontraksjOn **contraction**

Las contracciones ocurren durante el parto. ▸ Contractions happen during childbrith.

coordinación *n, f* • koorðinaθjOn, koorðinasjOn **coordination**

Era hermoso ver cómo se movían con tanta coordinación. ▸ It was beautiful to see how they moved with so much coordination.

corpulento/a *adj* • korpulento **hefty**

No eres nada corpulento. ▸ You're not hefty at all.

cuerpo *n, m* • kwerpo **body**

Leer no es menos imprescindible para nuestra mente de lo que comer es para nuestro cuerpo. ▸ Reading is not less necessary to our mind than food is to our body.

dañar *v* • daɲar **damage / harm / hurt**

Demasiada luz daña la vista. ▸ Too much light hurts the eye.

débil *adj* • dEβil **weak**

Se siente _débil_ después de su enfermedad. ▸ He feels _weak_ after his illness.

debilidad _n, f_ • deβiliðað   **weakness**

Un guerrero asimila su fortaleza y _debilidad_. ▸ The warrior is conscious of both his strength and his _weakness_.

debilitado/a _adj_ • deβilitaðo   **weakened**

Mi fuerza muscular se ha _debilitado_ por falta de ejercicio. ▸ My muscular strength has _weakened_ from lack of exercise.

debilitar _v_ • deβilitar   **to debilitate / to weaken**

Tantos días en el hospital la habían _debilitado_. ▸ So many days in hospital had _weakened_ her.

dedo _n, m_ • deðo   **finger**

Tengo una espina en el _dedo_ y no puedo sacármela. ▸ There's a thorn in my _finger_ and I can't get it out.

delgado/a _adj_ • delgaðo   **slim / thin**

Era muy alto y _delgado_, con piernas y brazos largos. ▸ He was very tall and _thin_, with long arms and legs.

dentadura _n, f_ • dentaðura   **dentition / dentures**

¿Necesito _dentadura_ postiza? ▸ Do I need _dentures_?

dental _adj_ • dental   **dental**

¿Tienes hilo dental? ▸ Do you have some dental floss?

dermatólogo *n, f/m* • dermatOloɣo **dermatologist**

Mi madre es dermatóloga. ▸ My mother is a dermatologist.

desaconsejar *v* • desakonsexaɾ **to advise against**

Yo quería viajar sola pero me lo desaconsejaron. ▸ I wanted to travel by myself but I was advised against it.

descansar *v* • deskansaɾ **to rest**

¿Puedo descansar un poco? ▸ Can I rest a bit?

desequilibrio *n, m* • desekiliβɾjo **instability / imbalance**

Ella tiene un desequilibrio hormonal. ▸ She has a hormonal imbalance.

desmayarse *v* • dezmajaɾse **to faint / to pass out**

Marta estaba a punto de desmayarse. ▸ Marta was about to faint.

desmayo *n, m* • dezmajo **faint / fainting**

Los desmayos son posibles síntomas. ▸ Fainting is a possible symptom.

despertar *v* • despeɾtaɾ **to awake / to wake up**

Logró despertar a Harry. ▸ He succeeded in waking Harry up.

deteriorar *v* • deteɾjoɾaɾ **to damage**

Ese producto te va a deteriorar el pelo. ▸ That product is going to damage your hair.

diarrea *n, f* • djarea   **diarrhea**

Necesito medicina para la diarrea. ▸ I need diarrhea medicine.

diente *n, m* • djente   **tooth**

Ese diente me duele. ▸ That tooth hurts.

dieta *n, f* • djeta   **diet**

Mi madre está a dieta. ▸ My mother is on a diet.

digerir *v* • dixerir   **to digest**

Hay frutas difíciles de digerir. ▸ There are fruits difficult to digest.

digestión *n, f* • dixestjOn   **digestion**

Dicen que beber un poco de vino ayuda a hacer la digestión. ▸ It is said that drinking a little wine aids digestion.

doler *v* • doler   **to ache / to hurt**

Te prometo que no te va a doler. ▸ It won't hurt, I promise.

dolor *n, m* • dolor   **ache / pain**

Me levanté hoy con dolor de cuello. ▸ I got up today with a pain in my neck.

dormido/a *adj* • dormiðo   **asleep**

Parece estar dormido. ▸ He seems to be asleep.

dormir *v* • doɾmiɾ **to sleep**

No podemos dormir por el ruido. ▸ We can't sleep because of the noise.

ejercicio *n, m* • exeɾθiθjo, exeɾsisjo **exercise**

Ese ejercicio es bueno para los músculos abdominales. ▸ That exercise is good for the abdominal muscles.

embarazada *adj* • embaɾaθaða, embaɾasaða **pregnant**

Estoy embarazada de cuatro meses. ▸ I am four months pregnant.

embarazo *n, m* • embaɾaθo, embaɾaso **pregnancy**

Hagamos un test de embarazo. ▸ Let's do a pregnancy test.

encía *n, f* • enθIa, ensIa **gum**

Los problemas de las encías son comunes. ▸ Gum problems are common.

energía *n, f* • eneɾxIa **energy**

¡Qué despilfarro de energía! ▸ What a waste of energy!

enfermar *v* • emfeɾmaɾ **to make ill / to fall ill**

Podemos enfermar en cualquier momento. ▸ We may fall ill at any moment.

enfermedad *n, f* • emfeɾmeðað **disease / illness / sickness**

A causa de su enfermedad él se vio obligado a dejar de fumar. ▸ Due to illness, he had to give up smoking.

enfermo/a adj • emfermo **ill**

Si no está enfermo, creo que vendrá. ‣ If he isn't ill, I think he will come.

enrojecer v • enroxeθer, enroxeser **to blush / to turn red**

Enrojeció cuando le hicieron esa pregunta. ‣ He turned red when he was asked that question.

equilibrado/a adj • ekiliβraðo **balanced**

¿Qué es una dieta equilibrada? ‣ What is a balanced diet?

equilibrar v • ekiliβrar **to balance**

¿Cómo puedo equilibrar la báscula? ‣ How can I balance the scale?

equilibrio n, m • ekiliβrjo **balance / equilibrium**

La vida es como montar en bicicleta: para mantenerte en equilibrio tienes que seguir moviéndote. ‣ Life is like riding a bicycle. To keep your balance you must keep moving.

especialista n, f/m • espeθjalista, espesjalista **expert / specialist**

Él tiene técnicas excelentes que sobrepasarían a un especialista. ‣ He has excellent techniques which would outdo a specialist.

esquelético/a adj • eskelEtiko **extremely thin**

Juana está esquelética. ‣ Juana is extremely thin.

estiramiento n, m • estiramjento **stretching**

89

Vamos a empezar con un poco de estiramientos. ▸ Let's start with some stretching.

estreñimiento *n, m* • estɾeɲimjento **constipation**

Necesito algo para el estreñimiento. ▸ I need something for constipation.

estrés *n, m* • estɾEs **stress**

Tengo manchas en la piel por el estrés. ▸ I have spots on my skin from stress.

farmacia *n, f* • faɾmaθja, faɾmasja **pharmacy / chemist's / drugstore**

Este medicamento todavía no se vende en las farmacias. ▸ This medicine is still not sold in pharmacies.

felicidad *n, f* • feliθiðað, felisiðað **happiness / joy**

La felicidad no puede comprarse. ▸ You cannot buy happiness.

fiebre *n, f* • fjeβɾe **fever / temperature**

Tengo tos y un poco de fiebre. ▸ I have a cough and a little fever.

forma *n, f* • foɾma **fit / shape**

¿Cómo puedes estar tan en forma? ▸ How can you be so fit?

fortalecer *v* • foɾtaleθeɾ, foɾtaleseɾ **to strengthen**

¿Cómo podríamos fortalecer nuestras habilidades? ▸ How could we strengthen our skills?

fractura *n, f* • fɾaktuɾa **break / fracture**

La fractura no fue tan grave como pensábamos. ▸ The fracture wasn't as serious as we thought.

fracturar v • frakturar   **to break / to fracture**

¿Cómo te fracturaste la rodilla? ▸ How did you break your knee?

frágil adj • frAxil   **fragile / frail**

Yo nunca dije que fuera frágil. ▸ I never said I was fragile.

frente n, f • frente   **forehead**

Él besó a su hija en la frente. ▸ He kissed his daughter on the forehead.

fresco/a adj • fresko   **cold / cool / fresh**

Por la mañana el aire es fresco. ▸ The air is fresh in the morning.

frescura n, f • freskura   **freshness / nerve**

La frescura es nuestra máxima prioridad. ▸ Freshness is our top priority.

frialdad n, f • frjaldað   **coldness**

No soporto la frialdad de esta casa. ▸ I can't stand the coldness in this house.

gordo/a adj • gorðo   **fat**

Estoy tan gordo que necesito ropa nueva. ▸ I'm so fat that I need new clothes.

gripe n, f • gripe   **flu / influenza**

Mi madre pilló la gripe la semana pasada. ▸ Last week my mother came down with the flu.

hidratar v • iðratar   **to hydrate / moisturize**

¿Qué usas para hidratarte la piel? ‣ What do you use to moisturize your skin?

hospital n, m • ospital   **hospital**

Ella continuamente entra y sale del hospital. ‣ She is constantly in and out of hospital.

huesudo/a adj • wesuðo   **bony**

¿Por qué es tan huesudo? ‣ Why is he so bony?

inconsciente adj • iŋkonsθjente, iŋkonssjente   **unconscious**

Ella está inconsciente. ‣ She is unconscious.

inflamar v • imflamar   **to inflame / to swell up**

¿Por qué se te inflamó la articulación? ‣ Why did your joint swell?

insomnio n, m • insomnjo   **insomnia**

¿Padece usted de insomnio? ‣ Do you suffer from insomnia?

lesionarse v • lesjonarse   **to get injured**

Los futbolistas se lesionan a menudo. ‣ Football players get injured often.

marearse v • marearse   **to feel dizzy / feel nauseated**

De pronto empecé a marearme. ▸ Sθddenly I felt dizzy.

medicación *n, f* ● meðikaθjOn, meðikasjOn   **medication**

Me he tomado la medicación. ▸ I have taken my medication.

médico de cabecera *n, f/m* ● mEðiko de kaβesera **general practitioner / family doctor**

Mi médico de cabecera es muy amable. ▸ My family doctor is very kind.

médico de familia *n, f/m* ● mEðiko de familja   **general practitioner / family doctor**

Deberías preguntar a tu médico de familia. ▸ You should ask your family doctor.

mental *adj* ● mental   **mental**

La salud mental es tan importante como la salud física. ▸ Mental health is as important as physical health.

mineral *n, m* ● mineral   **mineral**

Mi bebida habitual es zumo de manzana con agua mineral, pero el zumo de naranja también me gusta. ▸ My usual drink is apple juice with mineral water, but I also like orange juice.

miope *adj* ● mjope   **myopic / nearsighted**

¿Sabías que soy miope? ▸ Did you know I'm nearsighted?

miopía *n, f* ● mjopIa   **myopia / nearsightedness**

No considero mi miopía como un impedimento. ▸ I don't consider my myopia as an impediment.

mirada *n, f* • miɾaða   **look / glance**

La mirada en el rostro de mi jefe era severa. ▸ The look on my boss's face was severe.

morir *v* • moɾiɾ   **to die**

Al morir su marido, el bebé se convirtió en lo más importante para ella. ▸ After her husband died, her baby was all in all to her.

muela *n, f* • mwela   **molar**

Me tuvieron que sacar una muela. ▸ I had to get a molar extracted.

muñeca *n, f* • muɲeka   **wrist**

Me caí y me hice daño en la muñeca. ▸ I fell down and hurt my wrist.

musculoso/a *adj* • muskuloso   **brawny / muscular**

Él es alto y musculoso. ▸ He's tall and muscular.

muslo *n, m* • muzlo   **thigh**

Siento dolor en el muslo derecho. ▸ I feel pain in my right thigh.

nacer *v* • naθeɾ, naseɾ   **to be born**

Mi padre murió antes de nacer yo. ▸ My father died before I was born.

nocivo/a *adj* • noθiβo, nosiβo   **harmful**

Aquel producto es <u>nocivo</u>. ▸ That product is <u>harmful</u>.

oído *n, m* • oɪðo   **audition / ear / hearing**

Mi padre es tan viejo que es duro de <u>oído</u>. ▸ My father is so old that he is hard of <u>hearing</u>.

órgano *n, m* • Oɾɣano   **organ**

El cirujano le convenció para someterse a un trasplante de <u>órgano</u>. ▸ The surgeon persuaded him to undergo an <u>organ</u> transplant.

pastilla *n, f* • pastiʎa   **pill**

Tom se toma una <u>pastilla</u> con vitaminas y minerales todos los días. ▸ Tom takes a <u>pill</u> with vitamins and minerals every day.

pecho *n, m* • petʃo   **breast / chest**

Me duele el <u>pecho</u>. ▸ I have a <u>chest</u> pain.

pelo *n, m* • pelo   **hair**

Tengo el <u>pelo</u> marrón. ▸ I have brown <u>hair</u>.

pelo graso *n, m* • pelo ɡɾaso   **greasy hair / oily hair**

Necesitas un champú para <u>pelo graso</u>. ▸ You need shampoo for <u>greasy hair</u>.

pelo seco *n, m* • pelo seko   **dry hair**

Siempre he tenido el <u>pelo seco</u>. ▸ I've always had <u>dry hair</u>.

perjudicial *adj* • peɾxuðiθjal, peɾxuðisjal   **harmful**

Fumar es perjudicial para la salud. ▸ Smoking is harmful to your health.

peso *n, m* • peso   **weight**

Últimamente he perdido peso. ▸ I've lost weight recently.

piel *n, f* • pjel   **skin**

Los jabones aromáticos solían provocarle picor en la piel. ▸ Scented soaps tended to make her skin itch.

piel grasa *n, f* • pjel grasa   **oily skin**

La dermatóloga me dijo que tengo la piel grasa. ▸ The dermatologist told me I have oily skin.

piel mixta *n, f* • pjel miksta   **mixed skin / combination skin**

Mi hermana tiene la piel mixta. ▸ My sister has mixed skin.

piel seca *n, f* • pjel seka   **dry skin**

¿Cuál es la mejor crema para la piel seca? ▸ What's the best moisturizer for dry skin?

píldora *n, f* • pɪldora   **pill**

Una píldora para cada enfermedad. ▸ A pill for every ill.

pomada *n, f* • pomaða   **balm / cream / ointment**

Mis labios están resecos. Necesito pomada labial inmediatamente. ▸ My lips are dry. I need lip balm immediately.

precaución *n, f* • pɾekauθjOn, pɾekausjOn   **caution / precaution**

96

De aquí en adelante debemos ir con precaución. ▸ From this point, we must proceed with caution.

propiedades *n, f* • propjeðaðes   **properties**

Esta planta tiene propiedades curativas. ▸ This plant has healing properties.

proporción *n, f* • proporθjOn, proporsjOn   **proportion**

Se ha registrado una proporción baja de nacimientos. ▸ A low proportion of births has been registered.

recomendable *adj* • rekomendaβle   **advisable**

Es recomendable beber suficiente agua. ▸ It's advisable to drink plenty of water.

recomendación *n, f* • rekomendaθjOn, rekomendasjOn **recommendation**

Tu recomendación fue decisiva. ▸ Your recommendation made all the difference.

recomendar *v* • rekomendar   **to recommend**

Ya que nunca he comido aquí antes, no sé que recomendar. ▸ Since I've never eaten here before, I don't know what to recommend.

relajante *adj* • relaxante   **relaxant / relaxing / sedative**

Yo encuentro relajante el sonido de la lluvia. ▸ I find the sound of the rain relaxing.

remedio natural *n, m* • remeðjo natural   **natural remedy**

¿Qué piensas de los remedios naturales? ▸ What's your opinion about natural remedies?

reposo *n, m* • reposo   **repose / rest**

El médico dijo que será necesario hacer reposo después de la operación. ▸
The doctor said rest will be necessary after surgery.

resfriado *n, m* • resfɾjaðo   **cold**

Tengo un resfriado terrible. ▸ I have a terrible cold.

resfriarse *v* • resfɾjarse   **to catch a cold**

Él no quiere salir de la habitación por temor a volver a resfriarse. ▸ He doesn't
want to leave the room because he's afraid that he'll catch another cold.

resistencia *n, f* • resistenθja, resistensja   **endurance / resistance**

Admiro tu resistencia física. ▸ I admire your physical resistance.

respiración *n, f* • respiraθjOn, respirasjOn   **breath / breathing /
respiration**

Cuando se empieza a soñar, la respiración se vuelve irregular y menos pro-
funda. ▸ When dreams begin, breathing becomes irregular and less deep.

revisión *n, f* • reβisjOn   **check-up**

Yo recomiendo una revisión completa para tu esposo. ▸ I recommend a thor-
ough check-up for your husband.

rodilla *n, f* • roðiʎa   **knee**

Se golpeó la rodilla con la silla. ▸ He knocked his knee against the chair.

sangrar v • saŋgɾaɾ   **to bleed**

Su pierna herida empezó a sangrar de nuevo. ▸ His wounded leg began to bleed again.

sanitario adj, n, f/m • sanitaɾjo   **health / healthcare / nurse**

Hicieron un control sanitario. ▸ A health inspection was done.

sano/a adj • sano   **healthy**

Mi abuelo está muy sano. ▸ My grandfather is very healthy.

sonido n, m • soniðo   **sound**

El agua transmite mejor el sonido que el aire. ▸ Water transmits sound better than air.

sudar v • suðaɾ   **to sweat**

El ejercicio vigoroso te hace sudar. ▸ Vigorous exercise makes you sweat.

sudor n, m • suðoɾ   **perspiration / sweat**

Estábamos todos empapados de sudor. ▸ We were all drenched with perspiration.

termómetro n, m • teɾmOmetɾo   **thermometer**

El termómetro es un instrumento para medir la temperatura. ▸ The thermometer is an instrument for measuring temperature.

tirita n, f • tiɾita   **band-aid / plaster**

La herida dejó de dolerle cuando se puso una tirita. ▸ The wound stopped hurting after he put a band-aid on it.

tobillo *n, m* • toβiʎo   **ankle**

No voy a jugar porque me he torcido el tobillo. ▸ I won't play because I've twisted my ankle.

tomar *v* • tomaɾ   **to drink / to take**

Prefiero tomar una ducha por la mañana. ▸ I prefer to take a shower in the morning.

toser *v* • toseɾ   **to cough**

No puedo parar de toser. ▸ I can't stop coughing.

tronco *n, m* • troŋko   **trunk**

Las piernas están debajo del tronco. ▸ The legs are below the trunk.

vacuna *n, f* • bakuna   **vaccine**

Jonas Salk desarrolló la vacuna contra la polio en 1952. ▸ Jonas Salk developed the polio vaccine in 1952.

vigor *n, m* • biɣoɾ   **vigor**

Revivió con un vigor aún mayor. ▸ It revived with even greater vigor.

vigorizar *v* • biɣoɾiθaɾ, biɣoɾisaɾ   **to invigorate / to energize**

¿Cómo puedo vigorizar mi sistema inmunológico? ▸ How can I energize my immune system?

vigoroso/a *adj* • biɣoɾoso   **healthy / strong / vigorous**

Serás más <u>vigoroso</u> si te ejercitas. ▸ You will be more <u>vigorous</u> if you exercise.

5 Shopping

ahorrar *v* • aorar   **to save**

Ella está tratando de <u>ahorrar</u> todo lo posible. ▸ She is trying to <u>save</u> as much money as she can.

almacén *n, m* • almaθEn, almasEn   **storage / storehouse / warehouse**

Una vez que terminaron, las mercancías de la fábrica fueron transportadas al <u>almacén</u> para su almacenamiento. ▸ Once they were finished, goods from the factory were taken to the <u>warehouse</u> for storage.

artículo *n, m* • artIkulo   **article / item / object**

Este <u>artículo</u> es barato. ▸ This <u>article</u> is cheap.

asequible *adj* • asekiβle   **accessible / affordable / attainable**

Nuestros productos son <u>asequibles</u> para todos. ▸ Our products are <u>affordable</u> for everyone.

aumento *n, m* • aumento   **increase / rise**

Este extraordinario <u>aumento</u> se explica por la veloz unificación económica que tuvo lugar durante el mismo período. ▸ This extraordinary <u>increase</u> is explained by the speedy economic unification which took place during the same period.

bajada *n, f* • baxaða   **drop / reduction**

Se ha notado una bajada de precios generalizada. ▸ A general drop in prices has been noticed.

barato/a *adj* • barato   **cheap / inexpensive**

Cómprelo, es muy barato. ▸ Buy it, it's very cheap.

beneficio *n, m* • benefiθjo, benefisjo   **benefit / profit**

El mes pasado ganamos muy poco beneficio. ▸ We gained little benefit last month.

bolsa *n, f* • bolsa   **bag**

El ladrón se llevó mi bolsa. ▸ The thief ran off with my bag.

caja *n, f* • kaxa   **box / cash register / till**

El empleado robó dinero de la caja registradora. ▸ The employee stole money from the cash register.

calcular *v* • kalkular   **to calculate**

Yo no puedo calcular tan rápido como él. ▸ I can't calculate as fast as he.

calidad *n, f* • kaliðað   **quality**

Estos productos son de la misma calidad. ▸ These products are of the same quality.

calzado *n, m* • kalθaðo, kalsaðo   **footwear**

Es una especie de calzado. ▸ It's some kind of footwear.

cambio *n, m* • kambjo   **change**

Quiero hacer una llamada, pero no ando con <u>cambio</u>. ‣ I want to make a phone call, but I don't have any <u>change</u> now.

cargo *n, m* • kaɾɣo   **charge**

El precio del plato incluye un <u>cargo</u> por el servicio. ‣ The price of the meal includes a service <u>charge</u>.

carrito *n, m* • karito   **pram / stroller / cart**

Hay demasiadas cosas en este <u>carrito</u>. ‣ There are too many things in this shopping <u>cart</u>.

cartera *n, f* • kaɾteɾa   **wallet**

He buscado en todas partes pero no encuentro mi <u>cartera</u>. ‣ I've looked everywhere, but I can't find my <u>wallet</u>.

cesta *n, f* • θesta, sesta   **basket**

Ella tenía una <u>cesta</u> llena de manzanas. ‣ She had a <u>basket</u> full of apples.

cliente/a *n, m/f* • kljente   **customer**

El <u>cliente</u> no vino. ‣ The <u>customer</u> did not come.

cola *n, f* • kola   **line / queue**

Hay <u>colas</u> absurdas. ‣ There are insanely long <u>lines</u>.

comercial *adj* • komeɾθjal, komeɾsjal   **commercial**

Exportar es una actividad <u>comercial</u> que trasciende las fronteras. ‣ Exporting is a <u>commercial</u> activity which transcends borders.

comercio *n, m* • komeɾθjo, komeɾsjo   **business / store / trade**

Los ingleses entraron en el comercio del té en aquella época. ▸ The English entered into the tea trade at that time.

compraventa *n, f* • kompraβenta   **buying and selling / trade**

Trabajo en la compraventa de muebles. ▸ I work in the trade of furniture.

consumidor/a *n, f/m* • konsumiðoɾ   **consumer**

Si no reducen los impuestos al consumidor, no hay acuerdo. ▸ If you don't reduce consumer taxes, we've got no deal.

consumir *v* • konsumiɾ   **to consume / to use**

La fortaleza económica de un país reside no sólo en su capacidad de producir, sino también en su capacidad para consumir. ▸ The economic strength of a country lies not alone in its ability to produce, but also in its capacity to consume.

consumismo *n, m* • konsumizmo   **consumerism**

El consumismo ha aumentado en los últimos años. ▸ Consumerism has increased in the last years.

consumista *adj* • konsumista   **consumerist**

Hoy en día, vivimos en una sociedad consumista, y en consequencia, máquinas de coser se están convirtiendo obsoletas. ▸ Nowadays, we live in a consumerist society, and consequently, sewing machines are becoming obsolete.

crisis financiera *n, f* • kɾisis finansjeɾa   **financial crisis**

¿Cuándo terminará la crisis financiera? ▸ When will the financial crisis end?

departamento *n, m* • departamento   **department**

Él está a cargo del departamento de ventas. ▸ He's in charge of the sales department.

dependiente/a *n, m/f* • dependjente   **shop assistant / store clerk**

Trabajo como dependienta en este centro comercial. ▸ I work as a shop assistant in this shopping center.

derrochar *v* • derotʃar   **to squander / to waste**

Intento no derrochar el dinero. ▸ I try not to waste money.

descontar *v* • deskontar   **to discount**

Descontaron el 25% del precio final. ▸ They discounted 25% off the final price.

devolver *v* • deβolβer   **to give back / to return**

Él prometió devolver sin falta el dinero. ▸ He promised to return the money without fail.

dispositivo *n, m* • dispositiβo   **appliance / device**

Contáctese con la línea de servicio al cliente adecuada si el dispositivo no funciona apropiadamente. ▸ Contact the appropriate customer service helpline if the device does not operate properly.

diversión *n, f* • diβersjOn   **amusement / diversion / fun**

Ir de compras es divertido. ▸ It's fun to go shopping.

efectivo *n, m* • efektiβo   **cash**

Pagué esas compras en efectivo. ▸ I paid for the purchase in cash.

empaquetar *v* • empaketar   **to package / to wrap**

¿Has empaquetado todos los regalos? ▸ Did you wrap all the presents?

encontrar *v* • eŋkontrar   **to find**

Tenemos que encontrar un nuevo mercado para estos productos. ▸ We have to find a new market for these products.

entrada *n, f* • entraða   **entrance / entry / ticket**

Hemos quedado en la entrada. ▸ We're meeting at the entrance.

entrar *v* • entrar   **to enter**

Les he visto entrar en el banco. ▸ I saw them enter the bank.

entregar *v* • entreɣar   **to deliver / to hand over**

¿Han entregado ya el paquete? ▸ Have they already delivered the parcel?

envase *n, m* • embase   **container / packaging**

¿Qué hay dentro de este envase? ▸ What's inside this container?

enviar *v* • embjar   **to send / to ship**

Me gustaría saber cuándo lo puede enviar. ▸ I'd like to know when you can

<u>send</u> it out.

escaparate *n, m* • eskaparate   **shop window**

Me encanta todo lo que hay en este <u>escaparate</u>. ▸ I love everything in this <u>shop window</u>.

escaso/a *adj* • eskaso   **rare / scarce**

Los buenos trabajos son <u>escasos</u> últimamente. ▸ Good jobs are <u>scarce</u> lately.

especial *adj* • espeθjal, espesjal   **special**

El dinero se depositó en un fondo <u>especial</u> para comprar libros para la biblioteca de la escuela. ▸ The money was put into a <u>special</u> fund to buy books for the school library.

establecimiento *n, m* • estaβleθimjento, estaβlesimjento   **establishment**

¿Crees que ese restaurante es un buen <u>establecimiento</u>? ▸ Do you think that restaurant is a good <u>establishment</u>?

exportar *v* • eksportar   **to export**

¿<u>Exportan</u> muchos productos? ▸ Do they <u>export</u> many products?

factura *n, f* • faktura   **bill / invoice / receipt**

Mándeme la <u>factura</u> a casa. ▸ Send the <u>bill</u> to my house.

falsificación *n, f* • falsifikaθjOn, falsifikasjOn   **fake / falsification / forgery**

No compres esta pintura, es una <u>falsificación</u>. ▸ Don't buy this painting, it's a <u>fake</u>.

falsificar *v* • falsifikar   **to fake / to forge**

¿De verdad <u>falsificó</u> el certificado? ▸ Did she really <u>forge</u> the certificate?

fortuna *n, f* • fortuna   **fortune**

Fred dejó a su mujer una gran <u>fortuna</u>. ▸ Fred left his wife a large <u>fortune</u>.

ganga *n, f* • gaŋga   **bargain**

Este reloj es una verdadera <u>ganga</u>. ▸ This watch is a real <u>bargain</u>.

garantía *n, f* • garantІa   **guarantee / warranty**

Este televisor tiene dos años de <u>garantía</u>. ▸ This TV set has a two year <u>guarantee</u>.

gastar *v* • gastar   **to spend**

Puedes <u>gastar</u> este dinero como quieras. ▸ You may <u>spend</u> this money freely.

generoso/a *adj* • xeneroso   **generous**

Creo que soy bastante <u>generoso</u>. ▸ I think I'm pretty <u>generous</u>.

gerente *n, f/m* • xerente   **manager**

El <u>gerente</u> tiene muchos problemas. ▸ The <u>manager</u> deals with many problems.

grandes almacenes *n, m* • grandes almasenes   **department store**

Los compré en unos <u>grandes almacenes</u> de mi ciudad. ▸ I bought them in a department store of my city.

habitual *adj* • aβitwal   **regular / usual**

Soy un cliente habitual en un restaurante en este barrio. Vamos a comer hoy ahí. ▸ I'm a regular at a restaurant in this neighborhood. Let's have lunch there today.

hipermercado *n, m* • ipermeɾkaðo   **hypermarket / superstore**

¿Habéis estado en el nuevo hipermercado? ▸ Have you been to the new superstore?

horario *n, m* • oraɾjo   **time / timetable**

¿Sabes cuál es el horario de apertura de esta tienda? ▸ Do you know this shop's opening time?

hostelería *n, f* • osteleɾia   **hospitality**

Los trabajos de hostelería tienen muchos problemas debido a la pandemia. ▸ Hospitality jobs have many problems due to the pandemic.

importar *v* • impoɾtaɾ   **to import**

¿Crees que deberíamos importar arroz de los Estados Unidos? ▸ Do you think we should import rice from the U.S.?

imprescindible *adj* • impresθindiβle, impressindiβle   **essential / indispensable**

Un buen servicio de atención al cliente es imprescindible para mí. ▸ A good customer service is essential for me.

impuestos *n, m* • impwestos   **taxes**

Estoy muy a favor de bajar los impuestos. ▸ I'm very much in favor of cutting taxes.

incremento *n, m* • inkɾemento   **increase / rise**

Ha habido un gran incremento en comercio entre los Estados Unidos y China. ▸ There has been a large increase in trade between the United States and China.

ingreso *n, m* • iŋgɾeso   **deposit / income**

Esto ha incrementado el ingreso familiar. ▸ This has increased family income.

innecesario/a *adj* • inneθesaɾjo, innesesaɾjo   **pointless / unnecessary**

Te aseguro que es bastante innecesario. ▸ I assure you it's quite unnecessary.

intercambiar *v* • inteɾkambjaɾ   **to exchange / to trade**

Para las 5 de la tarde ya habían intercambiado todos los regalos. ▸ By 5 p.m. they had already exchanged all the presents.

inversión *n, f* • imbeɾsjOn   **investment**

Esta nueva inversión multiplicará nuestra ganancia. ▸ This new investment will multiply our profit.

invertir *v* • imbeɾtiɾ   **to invest**

Me intentaba convencer de invertir en aquel negocio. ▸ He was trying to convince me to invest in that business.

jefe/a *n, m/f* • xefe   **boss / head**

El jefe le hizo trabajar todo el día. ▸ He was made to work all day by the boss.

liquidación *n, f* • likiðaθjOn, likiðasjOn   **clearance / sale**

En aquel comercio hay una liquidación. ▸ There is a bargain sale at that store.

lleno/a *adj* • ʎeno   **crowded / full**

Lo sentimos, pero el día de hoy estamos llenos. ▸ Sorry, we're full today.

lujo *n, m* • luxo   **luxury**

En los Estados Unidos, el automóvil es una necesidad y no un lujo. ▸ In the United States the automobile is a necessity and not a luxury.

lujoso/a *adj* • luxoso   **luxurious**

¿De verdad quieres comprar un coche lujoso? ▸ Do you really want to buy a luxurious car?

malgastar *v* • malgastar   **to waste**

Mi madre me enseñó a no malgastar el dinero. ▸ My mother taught me not to waste money.

marca *n, f* • marka   **brand / make / trademark**

¿Cuál es tu marca de yogur favorita? ▸ What's your favorite brand of yogurt?

máximo/a *adj* • mAksimo   **maximum / at most**

Como máximo, costará diez pesos. ▸ At most, it'll cost ten pesos.

mínimo *n, m* • mÍnimo   **least / minimum**

Algunas plantas crecen bien con un mínimo de cuidado. ▸ Some plants grow well with a minimum of care.

modernizar *v* • moðerniθar, moðernisar   **to update / to revamp**

Me gustaría modernizar mi casa. ▸ I'd like to update my house.

moderno/a *adj* • moðerno   **modern**

Los muebles del salón eran de estilo moderno. ▸ The living room furniture was modern in style.

moneda *n, f* • moneða   **coin / currency**

Encontré una moneda en la acera. ▸ I found a coin on the sidewalk.

monedero *n, m* • moneðero   **purse**

Perdí mi monedero de camino a la escuela. ▸ I lost my purse on my way to school.

necesidad *n, f* • neθesiðað, nesesiðað   **necessity / need**

Ahora un computador es una absoluta necesidad. ▸ A computer is an absolute necessity now.

negocio *n, m* • neɣoθjo, neɣosjo   **business / deal / shop**

Invirtió todo su capital en ese negocio. ▸ He invested all his capital in that business.

oferta y demanda *n, f* • oferta i demanda   **supply and demand**

Como hombre de negocios, sabía que todo se basaba en la ley de la oferta y demanda. ▸ As a businessman, he knew everything was based on supply and demand.

pago *n, m* • payo   **pay / pay-off / payment**

El pago del coche se hará en 12 mensualidades. ▸ The payment for the car will be made in 12 monthly installments.

pedido *n, m* • peðiðo   **order**

Confirmé el pedido. ▸ I confirmed the order.

perder *v* • perðer   **to lose**

A menos que tomes una decisión rápido, vas a perder la oportunidad. ▸ Unless you make a decision quickly, the opportunity will be lost.

permitirse *v* • permitirse   **to afford**

Su padre puede permitirse el darle una gran paga cada mes. ▸ Her father can afford to give her a big allowance every month.

plazos *n, m* • plaθos, plasos   **installments**

Quiero pagar a plazos. ▸ I want to pay in installments.

pobre *adj* • poβre   **needy / poor**

Tú no sabes lo que es ser pobre. ▸ You don't know what it is to be poor.

porcentaje *n, m* • porθentaxe, porsentaxe   **percentage**

En muchos países los pobres pagan más impuestos como porcentaje de sus ingresos que los ricos. ▸ In many countries, the poor pay more taxes as a percentage of their income than the ricjh.

precioso/a *adj* • preθjoso, presjoso   **beautiful / gorgeous**

El dormitorio estaba repleto de adornos preciosos. ▸ The bedroom was laden with beautiful ornaments.

prenda *n, f* • prenda   **garment / piece of clothing**

¿Cuál es tu prenda de vestir favorita? ▸ What's your favorite piece of clothing?

probador *n, m* • proβaðor   **changing room**

Me robaron el monedero en el probador. ▸ I had my purse stolen in the changing room.

puesto *n, m* • pwesto   **position / stall / stand**

Siempre hay dinero en el puesto de plátanos. ▸ There's always money in the banana stand.

rastro *n, m* • rastro   **flea market / second-hand market**

¿Vamos al rastro el domingo? ▸ What about going to the flea market on Sunday?

rebaja *n, f* • reβaxa   **discount / sale**

El vendedor me hizo una rebaja en el precio del coche. ▸ The salesman gave me a discount on the car.

rebajado/a *adj* • reβaxaðo   **cheaper / reduced**

¿Está <u>rebajado</u> el precio de esta falda? ▸ Is the price of this skirt <u>reduced</u>?

rebajar v ● reβaxaɾ   **to discount / to reduce**

En agosto <u>rebajan</u> los precios. ▸ Prices are <u>reduced</u> in summer.

recibo n, m ● reθiβo, resiβo   **receipt**

Aquí está mi <u>recibo</u>. ▸ Here's my <u>receipt</u>.

rentable adj ● rentaβle   **profitable**

Él transformó su pequeño negocio familiar en una empresa altamente <u>rentable</u> con más de 200 empleados. ▸ He transformed his small family business into a highly <u>profitable</u> company with more than 200 employees.

rico/a adj ● riko   **rich / wealthy**

Si fuera <u>rico</u> lo compraría. ▸ If I were <u>rich</u>, I would buy it.

salida n, f ● saliða   **exit**

¿Dónde está la <u>salida</u>? ▸ Where is the <u>exit</u>?

sección n, f ● sekθjOn, seksjOn   **department / section**

Yo soy el encargado de la <u>sección</u> de libros. ▸ I'm in charge of the book <u>department</u>.

sector n, m ● sektoɾ   **sector**

El <u>sector</u> manufacturero está frenético con la nueva política monetaria. ▸ The manufacturing <u>sector</u> is a frenzy over the new monetary policy.

servicio n, m ● serβiθjo, serβisjo   **service**

La comida y el <u>servicio</u> son excelentes. ▸ The food and <u>service</u> are excellent.

subida *n, f* • suβiða   **climb / rise / upload**

¿Por qué rechazaste su petición de <u>subida</u> de sueldo? ▸ Why did you turn down his request for a pay <u>rise</u>?

subir *v* • suβiɾ   **to increase / to upload**

Desgraciadamente han <u>subido</u> el precio. ▸ Unfortunately they have <u>increased</u> the price.

tacaño/a *adj* • takaɲo   **mean / stingy**

No seas <u>tacaño</u>. ▸ Don't be <u>mean</u>.

talla *n, f* • taʎa   **size**

A ser posible, me gustaría cambiar esto por una <u>talla</u> más grande. ▸ If it's possible, I'd like to exchange this for a larger <u>size</u>.

tarjeta *n, f* • taɾxeta   **card**

He recibido tu <u>tarjeta</u>. ▸ I have received your <u>card</u>.

tarjeta de crédito *n, f* • taɾxeta de kɾEðito   **credit card**

¿Acepta <u>tarjeta de crédito</u>? ▸ Do you accept <u>credit cards</u>?

tarjeta de débito *n, f* • taɾxeta de dEβito   **debit card**

Sólo tengo una <u>tarjeta de débito</u>. ▸ I just have a <u>debit card</u>.

tienda de alimentación *n, f* • tjenda de alimentasjOn   **greengrocer's / grocery store**

¿Necesitas algo de la tienda de alimentación? ▸ Do you need anything from the grocery store?

tienda de comestibles *n, f* • tjenda de komestiβles   **greengrocer's / grocery store**

Voy a la tienda de comestibles a comprar pan. ▸ I'm going to the grocery to buy some bread.

tienda de ultramarinos *n, f* • tjenda de ultramarinos   **grocery**

La tienda de ultramarinos de mi barrio cerró el año pasado. ▸ The grocery in my neighborhood closed down last year.

transacción *n, f* • transakθjOn, transaksjOn   **deal / transaction**

¿Deseas hacer cualquier otra transacción? ▸ Do you wish to make any other transaction?

último/a *adj* • Ultimo   **final / last / latest / latter / ultimate**

Tengo una bicicleta de último modelo. ▸ I have a bicycle of the latest model.

valioso/a *adj* • baljoso   **valuable / worth**

Ella lleva puesto un valioso anillo. ▸ She is wearing a valuable ring.

valor *n, m* • balor   **courage / value**

El valor del dólar está subiendo. ▸ The value of the dollar is going up.

vendedor/a *n, f/m* • bendeðor **salesman / salesperson / seller / vendor**

Este vendedor insistía que le comprara un coche ▸ That salesman was persistent in asking me to buy a car.

vendedor/a ambulante *n, f/m* • bendeðoɾ ambulante   **peddler**

Mi tío era vendedor ambulante. ▸ My uncle was a peddler.

venta *n, f* • benta   **sale**

Estos artículos no están en venta. ▸ These articles are not for sale.

zapatería *n, f* • θapateɾIa, sapateɾIa   **shoe shop**

Miguel administra una zapatería. ▸ Miguel runs a shoe shop.

6 Sports & Hobbies

aburrimiento *n, m* • aβurimjento   **boredom**

El aburrimiento era lo que Aldous Huxley consideraba como una de las condiciones humanas más peligrosas. ▸ It was boredom that Aldous Huxley considered one of the most dangerous human conditions.

aburrirse *v* • aβurirse   **to get bored**

Tengo tantas cosas que hacer que nunca me aburro. ▸ I have so much to do that I never get bored.

acostumbrado/a *adj* • akostumbraðo   **used to**

No estoy acostumbrado a caminar distancias largas. ▸ I'm not used to walking long distances.

acostumbrarse *v* • akostumbrarse   **to get used to**

Uno puede acostumbrarse a todo. ▸ You can get used to anything.

activo/a *adj* • aktiβo   **active**

Estoy agradecido por los amigos que me mantienen activo y social. ▸ I am thankful for friends who keep me active and social.

aficionado/a *adj* • afiθjonaðo, afisjonaðo   **amateur / fan**

Soy aficionado al teatro. ▸ I am a fan of the theater.

agradable *adj* • aɣraðaβle   **enjoyable / nice / pleasant**

Nuestra visita ha sido muy agradable. ▸ Our visit has been very pleasant.

agradar *v* • aɣraðaɾ   **to please**

No sé cual es la clave del éxito, pero la clave del fracaso es intentar agradar a todo el mundo. ▸ I don't know the key to success, but the key to failure is trying to please everybody.

agrado *n, m* • aɣraðo   **liking / taste / kindness**

Espero que el vino sea de tu agrado. ▸ I hope the wine is to your taste.

alojamiento *n, m* • aloxamjento   **accommodation / housing / lodging**

El alojamiento es en tiendas individuales. ▸ Accommodation is in individual tents.

amante *n, f/m* • amante   **fan / lover**

Él es un amante del pan. ▸ He's a bread lover.

amistad *n, f* • amistað   **friendship**

Nuestra amistad va a durar mucho tiempo. ▸ Our friendship will last a long time.

apetecer *v* • apeteθeɾ, apeteseɾ   **to fancy / to feel like**

¿Qué os apetece hacer esta noche? ▸ What do you feel like doing tonight?

apoyar *v* • apojaɾ   **to support**

Estamos aquí para apoyarte. ▸ We are here to support you.

aprender v • aprender   **to learn**

Yo pensaba que te gustaba aprender cosas nuevas. ▸ I thought you liked to learn new things.

apuntarse v • apuntarse   **to sign up for**

Acabo de apuntarme al curso de español. ▸ I just signed up for the Spanish course.

árbitro n, m • Arβitro   **referee / umpire**

El árbitro sopló su silbato para terminar el partido. ▸ The referee blew his whistle to end the match.

arriesgado/a adj • arjezɣaðo   **adventurous / risky**

Yo pienso que es demasiado arriesgado. ▸ I think it's too risky.

atleta n, f/m • atleta   **athlete**

Ese atleta ganó el torneo tres veces seguidas. ▸ That athlete won three times in a row in this tournament.

atletismo n, m • atletizmo   **athletics**

Siempre estuve interesada en el atletismo. ▸ I've always been fond of athletics.

atreverse v • atreβerse   **to dare**

¿Te atreves a probar esta comida? ▸ Do you dare to try this food?

aventura n, f • aβentura   **adventure / affair**

Bill no tiene sentido de la aventura. ▸ Bill has no sense of adventure.

baile *n, m* • baile   **dance / dancing**

Tom no tenía intención de ir al baile con Mary. ▸ Tom had no intention of going to the dance with Mary.

boxeador *n, m* • bokseaðor   **boxer**

El boxeador tenía que perder peso para la pelea por el título. ▸ The boxer had to lose weight for the title match.

boxeo *n, m* • bokseo   **boxing**

Tenemos un club de boxeo en la escuela. ▸ We have a boxing club in our school.

bucear *v* • buθear, busear   **to dive**

Ella sabe bucear. ▸ She knows how to dive.

caballo *n, m* • kaβaʎo   **horse**

En esa carrera sólo compitieron cuatro caballos. ▸ Only four horses competed in the race.

caminar *v* • kaminar   **to walk**

Fue un día ideal para caminar. ▸ It was an ideal day for walking.

caminata *n, f* • kaminata   **hike / stroll/ walk**

No hay nada mejor que dar una buena caminata. ▸ There's nothing better than taking a nice walk.

campeón/a *n, f/m* • kampeOn   **champion**

Tiene el potencial para ser campeón del mundo. ► He has the potential to become world champion.

campeonato n, m • kampeonato   **championship / tournament**

Seguro que gana el campeonato de natación. ► He is sure to win the swimming championship.

carrera n, f • kareɾa   **race**

Me gustan las carreras de caballos. ► I like horse races.

charlar v • ʧaɾlaɾ   **to chat / to talk**

Me gustaría quedarme y charlar, pero tengo que irme a una reunión. ► I'd like to stay and chat, but I've got a meeting to go to.

chatear v • ʧateaɾ   **to chat**

Me gustaría chatear contigo por e-mail. ► I'd like to chat with you by e-mail.

ciclista n, f/m • θiklista, siklista   **cyclist**

Esquivé al ciclista por los pelos. ► I barely avoided the cyclist.

cinematográfico/a adj • θinematoɣɾAfikO, sinematoɣɾAfikO   **cinematographic**

Trabajamos en la industria cinematográfica. ► We work in the cinematographic industry.

colección n, f • kolekθjOn, koleksjOn   **assortment / collection**

125

Él me mostró su coleccíón de sellos. ▸ He showed me his stamp collection.

coleccionar *v* • kolekθjonaɾ, koleksjonaɾ   **to collect**

Mi hobby es coleccionar juguetes viejos. ▸ My hobby is to collect old toys.

coleccionista *n, f/m* • kolekθjonista, koleksjonista   **collector**

Este es un artículo de coleccionista. ▸ This is a collector's item.

competente *adj* • kompetente   **able / competent**

Era un poeta famoso y un diplomático competente. ▸ He was a famous poet and a competent diplomat.

componer *v* • komponeɾ   **compose / fix**

Nunca ha tenido el talento de componer melodías. ▸ He never had the talent of composing melodies.

concurso *n, m* • koŋkurso   **contest**

Le gustaría participar en el concurso. ▸ He would like to take part in the contest.

conseguir *v* • konseɣiɾ   **to achieve / to get**

¿Dónde puedo conseguir un mapa? ▸ Where can I get a map?

contrincante *n, f/m* • kontriŋkante   **competitor**

¿Podremos vencer a nuestros contrincantes? ▸ Will we be able to beat our competitors?

costumbre *n, f* • kostumbre   **convention / custom / habit / practice**

Papá tiene la costumbre de leer el periódico antes de desayunar. ▸ Father is in the habit of reading the paper before breakfast.

creatividad *n, f* • kɾeatiβiðað   **creativity**

La falta de inspiración es el peor enemigo de la creatividad. ▸ Lack of inspiration is the worst enemy of creativity.

creativo/a *n, f/m* • kɾeatiβo   **creative**

Si fuera más creativo, habría terminado hace horas. ▸ If I were more creative, I'd have finished hours ago.

crucigramas *n, m* • kɾuθiɣɾamas, kɾusiɣɾamas   **crossword**

¿Disfrutas con los crucigramas? ▸ Do you enjoy crosswords?

deporte *n, m* • depoɾte   **sport**

Un deporte de invierno con el que mucha gente disfruta es el patinaje. ▸ A winter sport that many people enjoy is ice skating.

derrota *n, f* • derota   **defeat / loss**

No nos interesan las posibilidades de derrota; no existen. ▸ We are not interested in the possibilities of defeat; they do not exist.

derrotar *v* • derotaɾ   **to beat / to defeat**

Puedo derrotar a cualquier jugador de ajedrez. ▸ I can defeat any chess player.

desafiar *v* • desafjaɾ   **to challenge**

127

Te desafío a un nuevo juego. ▸ I challenge you to a new game.

desafío *n, m* • desafĩo   **challenge / dare / defiance**

Me arriesgué y acepté su desafío. ▸ I took a chance and accepted his challenge.

descansar *v* • deskansar   **to rest**

Debes descansar después de hacer ejercicio. ▸ You should rest after exercise.

descanso *n, m* • deskanso   **break / rest**

Ya terminé toda mi tarea así que ahora me gustaría tomar un pequeño descanso. ▸ I have done all of my homework and I'd like to take a short break.

diversión *n, f* • diβersjOn   **amusement / diversion / fun**

Ella tenía tiempo para distraerse en su diversión favorita. ▸ She had time to lose herself in her favorite amusement.

divertido/a *adj* • diβertiðo   **amusing / fun / funny**

Me he divertido mucho. ▸ I had a lot of fun.

divertirse *v* • diβertirse   **to have fun**

Es más fácil divertirse que trabajar. ▸ It's easier to have fun than to work.

documental *n, m* • dokumental   **documentary**

Ese documental acerca de la crisis medioambiental me hizo abrir los ojos. ▸

That <u>documentary</u> about the environmental crisis was a real eye-opener.

elegir *v* • elexir **to choose**

Puedes <u>elegir</u> cualquiera de los dos libros. ▸ You may <u>choose</u> either of the two books.

enemistad *n, f* • enemistað **enmity / feud**

¿Qué causó la <u>enemistad</u> entre vosotros? ▸ What caused this <u>enmity</u> between you two?

enfrentarse *v* • emfrentarse **to confront / to face**

Ella estaba preparada para <u>enfrentarse</u> a su destino. ▸ She was ready to <u>face</u> her fate.

entrenador/a *n, f/m* • entrenaðor **coach / trainer**

Con un buen <u>entrenador</u>, el nadador lleva las de ganar. ▸ With a good <u>trainer</u>, the swimmer is bound to win.

entrenamiento *n, m* • entrenamjento **training / workout**

El <u>entrenamiento</u> es muy estricto. ▸ <u>Training</u> is really strict.

entrenar *v* • entrenar **to train / to work out**

¿Fue fácil <u>entrenar</u> a tu perro? ▸ Was it easy to <u>train</u> your dog?

entretener *v* • entretener **to amuse / to entertain**

Me <u>entretengo</u> viendo series de televisión. ▸ I <u>entertain</u> myself watching TV shows.

entretenido/a *adj* • entreteniðo **amusing / entertaining**

129

Este juego es muy entretenido. ▸ This game is very entertaining.

equilibrio *n, m* • ekiliβɾjo   **balance / equilibrium**

El equilibrio no es siempre fácil. ▸ Balance isn't always easy.

equipaje *n, m* • ekipaxe   **luggage**

No puedo encontrar mi equipaje. ▸ I can't find my luggage.

equipo *n, m* • ekipo   **team**

La elegimos a ella como capitana del equipo. ▸ We elected her captain of our team.

escalada *n, f* • eskalaða   **climbing / escalation**

Me encanta la escalada. ▸ I love climbing.

escalar *v* • eskalaɾ   **to climb / to scale**

Nos gustaría escalar esa montaña. ▸ We'd like to climb that mountain.

esquí *n, m* • eskI   **ski / skiing**

Quiero hacer esquí acuático. ▸ I want to water ski.

experimentar *v* • ekspeɾimentaɾ   **to experience / to experiment**

A Andrea le gusta experimentar. ▸ Andrea likes experimenting.

experto/a *adj* • ekspeɾto   **expert**

Él es experto en ordenadores. ▸ He is a computer expert.

exposición n, f • eksposiθjOn, eksposisjOn **display / exhibition**

¿Fuiste a la exposición de arte? ▸ Did you go to the art exhibition?

fascinación n, f • fasθinaθjOn, fassinasjOn **fascination / glamour**

Aprender idiomas es mi más grande fascinación y pasatiempo. ▸ Studying languages is my biggest fascination and hobby.

fascinante adj • fasθinante, fassinante **breathtaking / fascinating / intriguing**

Para mí, la historia es una asignatura fascinante. ▸ For me, history is a fascinating subject.

fascinar v • fasθinar, fassinar **to fascinate / to love**

Estoy fascinada por la flexibilidad de esta lengua. ▸ I'm fascinated by the flexibility of this language.

final adj/n • final **final / finale**

El marcador final fue de dos a cero. ▸ The final score was two to nothing.

fotografiar v • fotoɣrafjar **to photograph**

Voy a fotografiar los documentos. ▸ I'm going to photograph the documents.

fotográfico/a adj • fotoɣrAfiko **photographic**

¿Has visto este reportaje fotográfico? ▸ Have you seen this photographic report?

ganador/a *n, f/m* • ganaðoɾ   **winner**

Siempre fuiste un ganador. ▸ You were always a winner.

ganar *v* • ganaɾ   **to earn / to gain / to win**

Ella cumplió el objetivo de ganar el premio. ▸ She achieved the goal of winning the prize.

goleada *n, f* • goleaða   **hammering / rout**

El partido de fútbol terminó con una goleada de 9-0. ▸ The football match ended in a 9-0 rout.

grupal *adj* • gɾupal   **group**

Vamos a hacer una actividad grupal. ▸ Let's do a group activity.

habilidad *n, f* • aβiliðað   **ability / skill**

Nosotros tenemos la habilidad de recordar. ▸ We have the ability to remember.

habilidoso/a *adj* • aβiliðoso   **clever / skilled**

Le encantaría ser más habilidoso en su trabajo. ▸ He'd like to be more skilled in his work.

hípica *n, f* • Ipika   **equestrianism**

Siempre nos ha interesado la hípica. ▸ We've always had an interest in equestrianism.

incompetente *adj* • iŋkompetente   **incompetent**

Una gestión empresarial <u>incompetente</u> afecta directamente a los trabajadores.
▸ An <u>incompetent</u> business management directly affects the employees.

individual *adj* • indiβiðwal   **individual**

Cada niño tiene su modo <u>individual</u> de pensar. ▸ Each child has an <u>individual</u> way of thinking.

infantil *adj* • imfantil   **child-like / childish**

Es hora de que dejes tus costumbres <u>infantiles</u>. ▸ It is time you left off your <u>childish</u> ways.

interés *n, m* • interEs   **interest**

Ella parece no tener <u>interés</u> en el fútbol. ▸ She seems to have no <u>interest</u> in soccer.

interesante *adj* • interesante   **interesting**

El béisbol es un deporte <u>interesante</u>. ▸ Baseball is an <u>interesting</u> sport.

interesar *v* • interesar   **to get interested in / to interest**

Este asunto no me <u>interesa</u> en absoluto. ▸ This affair doesn't <u>interest</u> me at all.

juego *n, m* • xweyo   **game**

Ninguno de estos <u>juegos</u> es interesante. ▸ None of these <u>games</u> are interesting.

jugada *n, f* • xuyaða   **play / shot**

¿Podemos continuar la jugada? ▸ Can we continue the play?

jugador/a *n, f/m* • xuɣaðoɾ **player**

¿Cuál es la altura media de los jugadores? ▸ What is the average height of the players?

lograr *v* • loɣɾaɾ **accomplish / achieve / arrive / attain**

Él trabaja duro para lograr su objetivo. ▸ He works hard to achieve his goal.

luchador/a *n, f/m* • lutʃaðoɾ **fighter / wrestler**

Eres una auténtica luchadora. ▸ You're a real fighter.

marcar *v* • maɾkaɾ **to score**

¿Cuántos puntos marcaron? ▸ How many points did they score?

miembro *n, m* • mjembɾo **member**

Me hice miembro del club hace diez años. ▸ I became a member of the club ten years ago.

miniatura *n, f* • minjatuɾa **miniature / thumbnail**

La exposición de miniaturas fue un éxito. ▸ The exhibition of miniatures was a success.

musical *adj* • musikal **musical**

No todos nacemos con talento musical. ▸ Not all of us are born with musical talent.

natación *n, f* • nataθjOn, natasjOn **swimming**

Soy miembro del club de <u>natación</u>. ▸ I'm a member of the <u>swimming</u> club.

navegar por internet *v* • naβeɣaɾ poɾ internet   **to surf the internet**

¿Pasas mucho tiempo <u>navegando por internet</u>? ▸ Do you spend a long time surfing the internet?

obligación *n, f* • oβliɣaθjOn, oβliɣasjOn   **duty / obligation**

Es nuestra <u>obligación</u> ayudarles. ▸ It is our <u>duty</u> to help them.

organizar *v* • oɾɣaniθaɾ, oɾɣanisaɾ   **to organize**

Ayer nos coordinamos con nuestro jefe de facultad para <u>organizar</u> una fiesta en el edificio. ▸ Yesterday we coordinated with the department head to <u>organize</u> an office party.

pasatiempo *n, m* • pasatjempo   **hobby / pastime**

La pesca es mi <u>pasatiempo</u> preferido. ▸ Fishing is my favorite <u>hobby</u>.

pasear *v* • paseaɾ   **to stroll / to walk**

Me gusta <u>pasear</u> bajo la lluvia. ▸ I like to <u>walk</u> in the rain.

pasivo/a *adj* • pasiβo   **passive**

Él tiene un carácter <u>pasivo</u>. ▸ He has a <u>passive</u> character.

perdedor/a *n, f/m* • peɾðeðoɾ   **loser**

Confío en que, a la larga, no seré un <u>perdedor</u>. ▸ I trust that, in the long run, I will not be a <u>loser</u>.

perder *v* • peɾðeɾ   **to lose**

No hay tiempo que perder. ▸ There is no time to lose.

placentero/a *adj* • plaθentero, plasentero   **delightful / pleasant**

Fue muy placentero montar en moto. ▸ Riding a motorbike was quite pleasant.

placer *n, m* • plaθer, plaser   **delight / pleasure**

Algunas personas solo persiguen el placer. ▸ Some people pursue only pleasure.

polideportivo *n, m* • poliðeportiβo   **sports center**

No hay ni autobús no polideportivo. ▸ There are no buses and there isn't a sports center.

premio *n, m* • premjo   **award / premium / prize**

Diez equipos compitieron por conseguir el premio. ▸ Ten teams competed for the prize.

progreso *n, m* • proɣreso   **progress**

Este es un ejemplo del progreso que estamos haciendo. ▸ This is an example of the progress that we're making.

raqueta *n, f* • raketa   **racket**

¿Cuántas raquetas tiene? ▸ How many rackets do you have?

récord *n, m* • rEkorð   **record**

Él tiene un récord en natación. ▸ He holds a record in swimming.

red social *n, f* • reð sosjal   **social network**

¿Usas alguna red social? ▸ Do you use any social network?

reserva *n, f* • reserβa   **booking / reservation**

Me gustaría cambiar mi reserva. ▸ I'd like to change my reservation.

resultado *n, m* • resultaðo   **outcome / result**

Estaban satisfechos con el resultado. ▸ They were satisfied with the result.

retar *v* • retar   **to challenge**

¿Por qué crees que te retó? ▸ Why do you think she challenged you?

reto *n, m* • reto   **challenge / dare / reprimand**

¡Acepto el reto! ▸ I accept the challenge!

riesgo *n, m* • rjezɣo   **hazard / jeopardy / peril / risk**

¿Por qué asumes ese riesgo? ▸ Why do you take such a risk?

ritmo *n, m* • ritmo   **pace / rhythm**

Nunca se adaptó del todo al ritmo de la ciudad. ▸ He's never quite adjusted to the pace of the city.

saltar *v* • saltar   **to hop / to jump / to skip**

¿Cómo puedo saltar tan alto? ▸ How can I jump so high?

saltos *n, m* • saltos   **jump / leap**

Se vieron obligados a dar un salto para bajar rápido. ▸ They had to jump with a leap to be able to go down faster.

seguidor *n, f/m* • seɣiðoɾ   **fan / follower**

¿En serio eres seguidor de este equipo de baloncesto? ▸ Are you really a fan of this basketball team?

senderismo *n, m* • senderizmo   **hiking / trekking**

¿Por qué no os gusta el senderismo? ▸ Why don't you like hiking?

sentir *v* • sentiɾ   **to feel**

Sus palabras me hacen sentir mal. ▸ Your words make me feel bad.

teatral *adj* • teatral   **theatrical**

Su conducta era teatral. ▸ His behavior was theatrical.

televisivo/a *adj* • teleβisiβo   **television**

Nunca he visto este programa televisivo. ▸ I've never watched this television program.

tener ganas *v* • teneɾ ganas   **to fancy / to feel like**

Tengo ganas de ir al cine. ▸ I feel like going to the cinema.

tocar *v* • tokaɾ   **to play / to touch**

Suelo oírla tocar el piano. ▸ I often hear her play the piano.

turismo *n, m* • turizmo   **sightseeing / tourism**

El turismo creó muchos nuevos puestos de trabajo. ▸ Tourism generated many new jobs.

vacacional *adj* • bakaθjonal, bakasjonal   **holiday / vacation**

¿Cuál es vuestro destino vacacional preferido? ▸ What's your favorite holiday destination?

variedad *n, f* • barjeðað   **assortment / variety**

Había una gran variedad de platos en el menú. ▸ There was a great variety of dishes on the menu.

vela *n, f* • bela   **sail / sailing**

Me gusta cruzar el lago en barco de vela. ▸ I like to go across the lake in a sailboat.

vencer *v* • benθer, benser   **to beat / to defeat / to overcome**

Puedes vencer a la realidad con suficiente imaginación. ▸ Reality can be beaten with enough imagination.

viajero *n, f/m* • bjaxero   **traveller**

El viajero iba silbando por el bosque. ▸ The traveller went whistling through the forest.

victoria *n, f* • biktorja   **victory**

Felicitaciones por su victoria en el torneo. ▸ Let me congratulate you on your victory in the tournament.

videoconsola *n, f* • biðeokonsola   **video game console**

Estuvimos dos horas jugando a la videoconsola. ▸ We spent two hours playing with the game console.

videojuego *n, m* • biðeoxweɣo   **video game**

¿Si te diéramos un videojuego estarías contento? ▸ If we gave you a video game, would you be happy?

visitante *n, f/m* • bisitante   **visitor**

El niño ofreció una flor al visitante. ▸ The child offered a flower to the visitor.

vuelo *n, m* • bwelo   **flight**

El próximo vuelo sale a las 10:00. ▸ The next flight is at 10:00.

7

Education & Learning

academia *n, f* • akaðemja   **academy / school**

Estudiamos inglés en esta <u>academia</u> de idiomas. ▸ We study English in this languages <u>school</u>.

actividad extraescolar *n, f* • aktiβiðað ekstraeskolar   **extracurricular activity**

Nuestros maestros han planeado algunas <u>actividades extraescolares</u>. ▸ Our teachers have planned some <u>extracurricular activities</u>.

alumno *n, f/m* • alumno   **pupil / student**

Los libros de este <u>alumno</u> son nuevos. ▸ This <u>student</u>'s books are new.

ámbito *n, m* • Ambito   **field / scope / sphere**

Los traductores profesionales muy a menudo se especializan solo en un <u>ámbito</u>, por ejemplo derecho o medicina. ▸ Professional translators quite often specialize in just one <u>field</u>, for example law or medicine.

aprender *v* • aprender   **to learn**

Voy a la escuela porque quiero <u>aprender</u>. ▸ I go to school because I want to learn.

aprobar *v* • aproβaɾ   **to pass / to approve**

Tengo que aprobar este examen pase lo que pase. ▸ I must pass this exam, no matter what.

archivador *n, m* • aɾʧiβaðoɾ   **folder**

Pon estos documentos en el archivador, por favor. ▸ Please, put these documents in the folder.

argumento *n, m* • aɾɣumento   **argument / plot**

El argumento es riguroso y coherente pero a fin de cuentas poco convincente. ▸ The argument is rigorous and coherent but ultimately unconvincing.

asignatura *n, f* • asiɣnatuɾa   **subject**

El inglés se ha convertido en mi asignatura favorita. ▸ English has become my favorite subject.

asociación *n, f* • asoθjaθjones, asosjasjones   **association / group**

Soy miembro de una asociación científica. ▸ I'm a member of a scientific association.

atento/a *adj* • atento   **attentive / watchful**

Me pide que esté atento. ▸ He asks me to be attentive.

aula *n, f* • aula   **classroom**

Los niños ocuparon el aula grande y espaciosa. ▸ The children occupied the large and spacious classroom.

bachillerato *n, m* • baʧiʎerato   **A levels / High School Diploma**

El año pasado terminé el bachillerato. ▸ I finished high school last year.

beca *n, f* • beka   **grant / scholarship**

Es probable que consiga la beca. ▸ He is likely to win the scholarship.

biblioteca *n, f* • biβljoteka   **bookcase / library**

La biblioteca está en el segundo piso. ▸ The library is on the second floor.

bibliotecario *n, f/m* • biβljotekarjo   **librarian**

A Irene le gustaría ser bibliotecaria. ▸ Irene would like to be a librarian.

campus *n, m* • kampus   **campus**

¿Podrías enseñarme el campus? ▸ Could you show me the campus?

carpeta *n, f* • karpeta   **folder**

¿En qué carpeta guardaste el archivo? ▸ In which folder did you save the file?

carrera universitaria *n, f* • karera uniβersitarja   **university degree**

Nunca terminé la carrera universitaria. ▸ I never completed the university degree.

castigado/a *adj* • kastiɣaðo   **punished**

Será castigado. ▸ He shall be punished.

certificado *n, m* • θertifikaðo, sertifikaðo   **certificate**

Este es un certificado oficial. ▸ This is an official certificate.

ciencias *n, f* • θjenθjas, sjensjas   **sciences**

Las matemáticas son el fundamento de todas las ciencias. ▸ Mathematics are the foundation of all sciences.

colegio de primaria *n, f* • kolexjo de primarja   **primary school**

Somos maestras en este colegio de primaria. ▸ We are teachers at this primary school.

compañero/a de clase *n, m/f* • kompaɲero de klase   **classmates**

¿Cómo te estás llevando con tus nuevos compañeros de clase? ▸ How are you getting along with your new classmates?

componer *v* • komponer   **to compose / to form**

¿Has compuesto tú sola esta canción? ▸ Have you composed this song by yourlsef?

comprobar *v* • komproβar   **to check**

Primero debes comprobar que tu nombre está en la lista. ▸ You should check first if your name is on the list.

concentrarse *v* • konθentrarse, konsentrarse   **to concentrate / to focus**

Él trató de concentrarse en la carta. ▸ He tried to concentrate on the letter.

concluir *v* • konklwir   **to close / to conclude**

Todos tenéis que concluir vuestros escritos. ▸ You all need to close your compositions.

conferencia *n, f* • komfeɾenθja, komfeɾensja **conference / lecture / talk**

En definitiva, la conferencia internacional fue un suceso. ▸ All in all, the international conference was a success.

conocimiento *n, m* • konoθimjento, konosimjento **knowledge**

Tiene conocimientos de inglés. ▸ He has a knowledge of English.

considerable *adj* • konsiðeɾaβle **considerable**

Se estima que sus deudas ascenderán a una considerable suma. ▸ It is estimated that his debts will amount to a considerable sum.

continuar *v* • kontinwaɾ **to carry on / to continue**

Creo que deberíamos continuar esta conversación fuera. ▸ I think we should continue this conversation outside.

correcto/a *adj* • korekto **accurate / correct / right / righteous**

Me pregunto si lo que he escrito era correcto. ▸ I wonder if what I wrote was correct.

corregir *v* • korexiɾ **to amend / to correct**

A veces corregir es más difícil que escribir. ▸ Correcting is sometimes harder than writing.

curriculum *n, m* • kurikulum **curriculum**

¿Has presentado el curriculum en clase? ▸ Have you presented the curriculum in the class?

curso académico *n, m* • kuɾso akaðEmiko   **academic year**

Este año el curso académico empieza en octubre. ▸ This academic year begins in October.

derecho *n, m* • deɾetʃo   **law**

Él está estudiando derecho en la universidad. ▸ He is studying law at the university.

desarrollo *n, m* • desaroʎo   **development**

Estaba interesado sobre todo en el origen y desarrollo del universo. ▸ He was mainly interested in the origin and development of the universe.

descanso *n, m* • deskanso   **break / pause**

Reanudó su trabajo tras un breve descanso. ▸ He resumed his work after a short break.

desconcentrado/a *adj* • deskonθentɾaðo, deskonsentɾaðo   **distracted**

Perdona, hoy estoy desconcentrado. ▸ I'm sorry, I'm quite distracted today.

desobedecer *v* • desoβeðeθeɾ, desoβeðeseɾ   **to disobey**

Mi hijo me desobedeció cuando le pedí que llegara más temprano. ▸ My son disobeyed me when I asked him to come back earlier.

disciplina *n, f* • disθiplina, dissiplina   **discipline / subject**

La disciplina es el componente más importante del éxito. ▸ Discipline is the most important part of success.

disciplinado/a *adj* • disθiplinaðo, dissiplinaðo   **disciplined /**
well-behaved

Carolina no es lo suficientemente disciplinada. ▸ Carolina is not disciplined
enough.

disciplinar *v* • disθiplinar, dissiplinar   **to discipline**

Intentamos disciplinar al niño pero fue imposible. ▸ We tried to discipline
the child but it was impossible.

distraído/a *adj* • distraIðo   **absent / distracted**

¡Obviamente estaba un poco distraído! ▸ I was obviously a little distracted!

doctorado *n, m* • doktoraðo   **doctorate / PhD**

Será un gran desafío ingresar al doctorado. ▸ Entering the doctorate is going
to be a great challenge.

doctrina *n, f* • doktrina   **doctrine / teaching**

El nihilismo es una doctrina filosófica. ▸ Nihilism is a philosophical doctrine.

duración *n, f* • duraθjOn, durasjOn   **duration**

¿Conoces la duración del examen de lengua? ▸ Do you know the duration
of the language exam?

educación infantil *n, f* • eðukasjOn imfantil   **pre-school**

Empecé la educación infantil cuando tenía 4 años. ▸ I started pre-school when I was 4.

educar v • eðukar   **to educate / to school**

¿Cómo deberíamos educar a nuestros hijos? ▸ How should we educate our children?

educativo/a adj • eðukatiβo   **educational**

Hablamos del asunto desde un punto de vista educativo. ▸ We discussed the matter from an educational point of view.

enfocarse v • emfokarse   **to focus**

Tienes que enfocarte todo lo posible o suspenderás. ▸ You have to focus as much as possible or you'll fail.

enseñar v • ensejñar   **to teach**

Nunca me ha gustado la forma de enseñar las lenguas extranjeras en la escuela. ▸ I've never liked the way foreign languages were taught at school.

época n, f • Epoka   **age / period / time**

Mis abuelos siempre estuvieron adelantados a su época. ▸ My grandparents were always ahead of their time.

escolar adj • eskolar   **academic / scholastic / schoolchild**

El curso escolar ha terminado. ▸ The academic year is over.

esquema n, m • eskema   **diagram / scheme**

Este esquema de las partes del cuerpo es muy útil. ▸ This diagram of the parts of the body is very useful.

estilo *n, m* • estilo **style**

El estilo es para el escritor lo que el color para el pintor. ▸ Style is to the writer what color is to the painter.

estresante *adj* • estresante **stressful**

El periodo de exámenes fue muy estresante. ▸ The exams period was very stressful.

examen escrito *n, m* • eksamen eskrito **written exam**

¿Va a ser un examen escrito? ▸ Is it going to be a written exam?

examen oral *n, m* • eksamen oral **oral exam**

Me estreso mucho en los exámenes orales. ▸ I get stressed out in oral exams.

excursión *n, f* • ekskursjOn **excursion / trip**

Marco y Laura se conocieron en una excursión a la montaña. ▸ Marco and Laura met each other on a day trip to the mountain.

expediente *n, m* • ekspeðjente **record**

Ese estudiante tiene el mejor expediente académico del año. ▸ That student has the best academic record of the year.

experto/a *n, f/m* • eksperto **expert**

Él es un experto en astronomía. ▸ He is an expert in astronomy.

extensión *n, f* • ekstensjOn **extension / extent / length**

¿Cuál es la extensión del archivo? ▸ What is the file extension?

facultad *n, f* • fakultað   **college / faculty / school**

Él es ahora estudiante de la facultad. ▸ He's now a college student.

física *n, f* • fIsika   **physics**

Esto plantea un problema interesante para teorías clásicas de la física. ▸ This poses an interesting problem for classical theories of physics.

folio *n, m* • foljo   **sheet**

¡Coge un folio y escribe! ▸ Take a sheet of paper and write!

forma *n, f* • forma   **form / kind / manner / shape / way**

No me gusta la forma en que él habla. ▸ I don't like the way he talks.

grado *n, m* • graðo   **degree / grade / rank / year**

Con un grado universitario, Tom conseguirá un mejor empleo. ▸ Tom will get a better job with a college degree.

graduado/a *n, f/m* • graðwaðo   **graduate**

Espero sacarme el graduado universitario la próxima primavera. ▸ I hope to graduate from university next spring.

guardería *n, f* • gwarðerIa   **daycare center / nursery school**

Mi hija va a la guardería tres veces por semana. ▸ My daughter goes to nursery three times per week.

histórico/a *adj* • istOriko   **historic / historical**

La caída del muro de Berlín fue un acontecimiento histórico. ▸ The falling of the Berlin Wall was a historic event.

humanidades *n, f* • umaniðaðes   **arts / humanities**

La historia es una rama de las humanidades. ▸ History is a branch of the humanities.

idiomas *n, m* • iðjomas   **languages**

Me gusta estudiar idiomas extranjeros. ▸ I like to study foreign languages.

incremento *n, m* • inkremento   **increase / rise**

El incremento del conocimiento científico es imparable. ▸ The increase of scientific knowledge is unstoppable.

inexperto/a *adj* • ineksperto   **inexperienced**

Sus errores se deben a que todavía es inexperto en este campo. ▸ His mistakes have to do with him being still inexperienced in this field.

informática *n, f* • imformAtika   **information technology / computer science**

Mi hijo quiere estudiar informática. ▸ My son wants to study computer science.

inglés *n, m / adj* • iŋglEs   **English**

Escribí una carta en inglés. ▸ I wrote a letter in English.

inmaduro/a *adj* • immaðuro   **immature**

Él es joven e <u>inmaduro</u>. ▸ He's young and <u>immature</u>.

institución *n, f* • instituθjOn, institusjOn   **institution**

Esta es una <u>institución</u> académica seria. ▸ This is a serious academic <u>institution</u>.

instituto *n, n* • instituto   **academy / institute / school**

Él ha estado jugando al ajedrez desde que estaba en el <u>instituto</u>. ▸ He has been playing chess since he was in high <u>school</u>.

instituto de secundaria *n, m* • insituto de sekundarja   **high school / secondary school**

Terminé el <u>instituto de secundaria</u> el año pasado. ▸ I finished the <u>secondary school</u> last year.

inteligente *adj* • intelixente   **bright / intelligent / smart**

El niño era sumamente <u>inteligente</u>. ▸ The child was exceptionally <u>intelligent</u>.

lengua *n, f* • leŋgwa   **language / tongue**

Es una buena idea estudiar la <u>lengua</u> y cultura del país que vas a visitar. ▸ It's a good idea to study the <u>language</u> and culture of the country you're going to visit.

lenguaje *n, m* • leŋgwaxe   **language**

¿Necesitamos un <u>lenguaje</u> universal? ▸ Do we need a universal <u>language</u>?

licenciado/a *n, f/m* • liθenθjaðo, lisensjaðo   **graduate**

¿En qué universidad te has <u>licenciado</u>? ▸ Which university have you graduated from?

licenciatura *n, f* • liθenθjatura, lisensjatura   **bachelor's degree / degree**

Tengo una licenciatura en biología. ‣ I have a degree in biology.

listo/a *adj* • listo   **clever / smart / ready**

Él no es menos listo que su padre. ‣ He is not less clever than his father is.

maduro/a *adj* • maðuro   **mature**

Él quiere parecer más maduro de lo que es. ‣ He wants to look more mature than he is.

maestro/a *n, f/m* • maestro   **teacher**

El grupo consistía de maestros y alumnos. ‣ The group was made up of teachers and students.

máster *n, m* • mAster   **master**

Mi hermano tiene un máster en Economía. ‣ My brother has a Master's degree in Economics.

materia *n, f* • materja   **content / matter / subject**

¿Cuál es tu materia favorita? ‣ Which subject do you like best?

matrícula *n, f* • matrIkula   **enrollment / registration**

Tengo que pagar la matrícula antes de que empiece el curso. ‣ I have to pay the enrollment before the course starts.

matricularse *v* • matrikularse   **to enroll / to register**

Mi hermana es poco previsora y se ha olvidado de matricularse en el curso.
▸ My sister is not very organized and forgot to register for the course.

memoria *n, f* • memoɾja   **memoir / memory / remembrance**

Me gustaría encontrar la manera de mejorar mi memoria. ▸ I'd like to find
a way to improve my memory.

memorizar *v* • memoɾiθaɾ, memoɾisaɾ   **to memorize**

¿Conoces algún buen método de memorizar vocabulario nuevo? ▸ Do you
know a good way to memorize new vocabulary?

modificar *v* • moðifikaɾ   **to alter / to change / to modify**

¿Cómo puedo modificar esta frase? ▸ How can I change this sentence?

modo *n, m* • moðo   **manner / way**

Lo apuntaremos del siguiente modo. ▸ We'll note it in the following way.

necesidad *n, f* • neθesiðað, nesesiðað   **need**

Las personas tienden a subestimar sus necesidades futuras. ▸ People have
a tendency to underestimate their future needs.

nivel *n, m* • niβel   **level**

¿Cuándo alcanzaremos un nivel de lengua más alto? ▸ When will we reach
a higher language level?

nota *n, f* • nota   **grade / mark / note**

No puedes sacar una buena nota sin trabajar duro. ▸ You cannot make a good mark without working hard.

obedecer v • oβeðeθer, oβeðeser   **to obey**

Debes aprender a obedecer instrucciones. ▸ You must learn to obey instructions.

obediencia n, f • oβeðjenθja, oβeðjensja   **obedience**

La obediencia es prioritaria en este colegio. ▸ Obedience is a priority in this school.

obediente adj • oβeðjente   **obedient**

Estos niños no son obedientes. ▸ These children are not obedient.

obligatorio/a adj • oβliɣatorjo   **compulsory / mandatory**

¿Es verdad que esta asignatura es obligatoria? ▸ Is it true that this subject is mandatory?

observador/a adj • oβserβaðor   **alert / observant / watchful**

Esa niña es muy observadora, ¿no crees? ▸ That girl is very observant, don't you think?

observar v • oβserβar   **to observe / to watch**

Nos interesa observar las costumbres de las diferentes regiones. ▸ We're interested in observing the customs of different regions.

olvidadizo/a adj • olβiðaðiθo, olβiðaðiso   **forgetful**

No soy olvidadizo. ▸ I'm not forgetful.

olvidar v • olβiðar   **to forget**

¿Es más difícil perdonar u <u>olvidar</u>? ▸ Is it harder to forgive or to <u>forget</u>?

opcional *adj* • opθjonal, opsjonal   **optional**

¿Has elegido ya los módulos <u>opcionales</u> del curso? ▸ Have you already chosen the <u>optional</u> modules of the course?

optativo/a *adj* • optatiβo   **optional**

Tengo tres asignaturas <u>optativas</u>. ▸ I have three <u>optional</u> subjects.

ortografía *n, f* • ortoɣrafĺa   **orthography / spelling**

Su redacción está muy bien, excepto por un par de errores de <u>ortografía</u>. ▸ Her composition is very good except for two <u>spelling</u> errors.

ortográfico/a *adj* • ortoɣrAfiko   **orthographic / orthographical / spelling**

¿Usas el corrector <u>ortográfico</u> en tu móvil? ▸ Do you use the <u>spell</u> checker of your mobile?

patio *n, m* • patjo   **playground / patio / yard**

Los niños están corriendo en el <u>patio</u>. ▸ Children are running in the <u>playground</u>.

pensar *v* • pensar   **to think**

Déjame <u>pensar</u> un momento. ▸ Let me <u>think</u> for a minute.

pizarra *n, f* • piθara, pisara   **board / blackboard / chalkboard / whiteboard**

El maestro escribió su nombre en la <u>pizarra</u>. ▸ The teacher wrote his name on the blackboard.

plan *n, m* • plan   **plan**

Yo estaba de acuerdo con su plan. ‣ I agreed with his plan.

precisar *v* • preθisar, presisar   **to specify**

Ella precisó que el artículo no era suyo. ‣ She specified that the article wasn't hers.

precisión *n, f* • preθisjOn, presisjOn   **accuracy / precision**

La precisión es importante en aritmética. ‣ Accuracy is important in arithmetic.

preciso/a *adj* • preθiso, presiso   **accurate / precise / to the point**

Sé más precisa. ‣ Be more precise.

primaria *n, f* • primarja   **elementary / primary**

Este problema es demasiado complicado como para que lo resuelvan estudiantes de primaria. ‣ This problem is too difficult for primary school children to solve.

principio *n, m* • prinθipjo, prinsipjo   **beginning / principle**

Empecemos por el principio. ‣ Let's start from the beginning.

prioritario/a *adj* • prjoritarjo   **critical / imperative**

Es prioritario informar a los padres de los alumnos. ‣ It's imperative to inform students'parents.

privilegiado/a *adj* • priβilexjaðo   **privileged / extraordinary**

Tienes una memoria privilegiada. ▸ You have an extraordinary memory.

privilegio *n, m* • priβilexjo   **privilege**

Él tuvo el privilegio de una educación privada. ▸ He had the privilege of a private education.

programa de estudios *n, m* • proɣrama de estuðjos   **syllabus**

Esta asignatura no es parte del programa de estudios de este trimestre. ▸ This subject is not part of this term syllabus.

progreso *n, m* • proɣreso   **progress**

No puede haber progreso sin comunicación. ▸ There cannot be progress without communication.

prueba *n, f* • prweβa   **evidence / proof / test / trial**

Él pudo nadar lo suficientemente rápido para pasar la prueba. ▸ He could swim fast enough to pass the test.

recordar *v* • rekorðaɾ   **to recall / to remember / to remind**

Una buena contraseña debería ser difícil de adivinar pero fácil de recordar. ▸ A good password should be difficult to guess, but easy to remember.

recreo *n, m* • rekreo   **break / recess / playground**

Se acabó el recreo. ▸ Recess ended.

regla *n, f* • reɣla   **rule / ruler**

Jugamos según las nuevas reglas. ▸ We played the game in accordance with the new rules.

repetir *v* • repetir   **to repeat**

El profesor me hizo repetir la oración. ▸ The teacher made me repeat the sentence.

resumir *v* • resumir   **to outline / to summarize**

La profesora nos dijo que resumiéramos el artículo. ▸ The teacher told us to summarize the article.

ruidoso/a *adj* • rwiðoso   **loud / noisy**

No seas tan ruidoso, por favor. ▸ Don't be so noisy, please.

secretaría *n, f* • sekretaria   **secretary's office**

Debemos mandar esos documentos a la secretaría de la facultad. ▸ We must send those documents to the secretary's office of the faculty.

secundaria *n, f* • sekundarja   **secondary school / high school**

Abandoné la escuela secundaria a los dieciséis. ▸ I dropped out of high school when I was sixteen.

selectividad *n, f* • selektiβiðað   **university entrance exam**

¿Qué sacaste en la selectividad? ▸ What did you get on the university entrance exam?

silencioso/a *adj* • silenθjoso, silensjoso   **quiet / silent**

Cuanto más silencioso seas, más serás capaz de escuchar. ▸ The quieter you become, the more you are able to hear.

sobresaliente *adj* • soβresaljente   **excellent / outstanding**

Habéis hecho un trabajo sobresaliente. ▸ You've done an outstanding job.

soñador/a *n, f/m* • soɲaðor   **dreamer**

Todo gran descubridor ha sido considerado como un soñador. ▸ All great discoverers have been regarded as dreamers.

soñar *v* • soɲar   **to dream**

Yo solía soñar con ser millonario. ▸ I used to dream about being a millionaire.

subrayar *v* • suβrajar   **to emphasize / to underline**

Subrayad las palabras que no sepáis. ▸ Underline the words that you don't know.

sueño *n, m* • sweɲo   **dream**

Algún día mi sueño se hará realidad. ▸ Some day my dream will come true.

suspender *v* • suspender   **to cancel / to fail**

Él entró en la universidad tras haber suspendido dos veces. ▸ He entered the university after failing the examination twice.

suspenso *n, m* • suspenso   **fail / failing grade**

Saqué un suspenso en el último examen. ▸ I was given a fail in the last test.

tachar *v* • taʧar   **to cross out**

Deberías tachar las palabras que no necesites. ▸ You should cross out any word you don't need.

término *n, m* • tЕrmino   **term**

"Radiactividad" es un término químico. ▸ 'Radioactivity' is a chemistry term.

terminología *n, f* • terminoloxIa   **terminology**

No sé nada de terminología legal. ▸ I don't know anything about legal terminology.

tesis doctoral *n, f* • tesis doktoral   **doctoral thesis**

Me llevó cinco años terminar la tesis doctoral. ▸ It took me five years to finish my doctoral thesis.

trimestre *n, m* • trimestre   **term / trimester**

Tus calificaciones estaban muy debajo del promedio este trimestre. ▸ Your marks were well below average this term.

tutor/a *n, f/m* • tutor   **guardian / tutor**

Como estudiante de doctorado, estaba muy contento con mi tutora. ▸ As a PhD student, I was quite happy with my tutor.

tutoría *n, f* • tutorIa   **tutorial**

Aprendimos mucho en las tutorías de internet de esta escuela. ▸ We learnt a lot in the online tutorials of this school.

últimos *adj* • Ultimos   **last / last one**

Dame cinco minutos para completar los últimos ajustes. ▸ Give me five minutes to finish the last adjustments.

uniforme *n, m* • uniforme   **uniform**

Todos vestían uniforme. ▸ They were all dressed in uniforms.

vago/a *adj* • bayo   **lazy**

O no sabe cómo lavar los platos o es que es muy vago. ▸ Either he doesn't know how to wash the dishes or he is just lazy.

8 Art & History

abstracto/a *adj* • aβstrakto   **abstract**

El arte abstracto no es del gusto de todos. ▸ Abstract art is not to the taste of everyone.

antigüedad *n, f* • antiɣweðað   **ancient times / antique / antiquity**

Los héroes de la antigüedad estaban dotados de muchas virtudes. ▸ The ancient heroes were all endowed with many virtues.

antiguo/a *adj* • antiɣwo   **ancient / old**

Es el edificio de madera más antiguo que existe. ▸ It is the oldest wooden building in existence.

armonía *n, f* • armonIa   **harmony**

La falta de armonía entre los colores hace que esta pintura resalte. ▸ The lack of harmony between colors makes this painting stand out.

armonioso/a *adj* • armonjoso   **harmonious**

Me encanta esta pintura por sus harmoniosos colores. ▸ I love this painting because of its harmonious colors.

arquitectónico/a *adj* • arkitektOniko   **architectural**

Estos edificios conservan un estilo arquitectónico único. ▸ These buildings conserve a unique architectural style.

arquitectura *n, f* • aɾkitektuɾa   **architecture**

Ha habido mucha discusión últimamente sobre la arquitectura de la nueva escuela. ▸ There was a lot of talk lately about the architecture of the new school.

artista *n, f/m* • aɾtista   **artist / performer / star**

El pobre joven finalmente se convirtió en un gran artista. ▸ The poor young man finally became a great artist.

autor/a *n, f/m* • autoɾ   **author**

Es un autor famoso por sus novelas y cuentos. ▸ He is an author famous for his novels and stories.

bellas artes *n, f* • beʎas aɾtes   **fine arts**

Siempre quise ingresar en la Academia de Bellas Artes. ▸ I always wanted to enter the Academy of Fine Arts.

biblioteca *n, f* • biβljoteka   **bookcase / library**

Disculpe ¿Me puede decir dónde está la biblioteca? ▸ Excuse me, can you tell me the way to the library?

bronce *n, m* • bɾonθe, bɾonse   **bronze**

El bronce está compuesto de cobre y estaño. ▸ Bronze is composed of copper and tin.

capilla *n, f* • kapiʎa   **chapel**

La Capilla Sixtina es una enorme capilla construida en el Palacio del Vaticano en 1473. ▸ The Sistine Chapel is a vast chapel built inside the Vatican Palace in 1473.

carbón *n, m* • kaɾβOn   **carbon / charcoal / coal**

El cuervo es tan negro como el carbón. ▸ The raven is as black as coal.

castillo *n, m* • kastiʎo   **castle**

Creo que el castillo de Malbork es una maravilla. ▸ I think Malbork castle is wonderful.

caverna *n, f* • kaβeɾna   **cavern**

Encontramos una caverna durante nuestra excursión. ▸ We found a cavern during our day trip.

cineasta *n, f/m* • θineasta, sineasta   **filmmaker**

Él fue un famoso cineasta italiano. ▸ He was a famous Italian filmmaker.

civilización *n, f* • θiβiliθaθjOn, siβilisasjOn   **civilization**

Descubrimos ruinas de una civilización antigua. ▸ We discovered relics of an ancient civilization.

civilizado/a *adj* • θiβiliθaðo, siβilisaðo   **civilized**

¿Podrías ser un poco más civilizado? ▸ Could you be a bit more civilized?

civilizar *v* • θiβiliθaɾ, siβilisaɾ   **to civilize**

Los romanos trataron de civilizar a los antiguos bretones. ▸ The Romans tried to civilize the ancient Britons.

colores cálidos *n, m* • koloɾes kAliðos   **warm colors**

Vamos a pintar el salón de colores cálidos. ▸ We're going to paint the living room in warm colors.

colores fríos *n, m* • koloɾes fɾIos   **cold colors**

EL azul es, sin duda, un color frío. ▸ No doubt blue is a cold color.

colorido/a *adj* • koloɾiðo   **color / coloring**

Ella descubrió un nuevo y colorido mundo. ▸ She discovered a colourful new world.

comienzo *n, m* • komjenθo, komjenso   **beginning / start**

La filosofía moderna tiene su comienzo en el siglo XIX. ▸ Modern philosophy has its beginnings in the 19th century.

concretar *v* • konkɾetaɾ   **to sum up / to specify**

Tus ideas son muy generales, ¿puedes concretar? ▸ Your ideas are too vague, can you specify?

concreto/a *adj* • konkɾeto   **specific**

Un escritor efectivo es aquél que sabe qué clase de palabras deben usarse en un contexto concreto. ▸ An effective writer is one who knows what sort of words should be employed in any specific context.

conocer *v* • konoθeɾ, konoseɾ   **to know**

¿Quién no conoce un proverbio tan simple? ▸ Who doesn't know such a simple proverb?

construir *v* • konstɾwiɾ   **to build**

El puente lo <u>construyeron</u> los romanos. ▸ The bridge was <u>built</u> by the Romans.

copia *n, f* • kopja   **copy**

Compara la <u>copia</u> con el original. ▸ Compare the <u>copy</u> with the original.

copiar *v* • kopjaɾ   **to copy**

Traducir se parece mucho a <u>copiar</u> pinturas. ▸ Translation is very much like <u>copying</u> paintings.

costumbre *n, f* • kostumbɾe   **custom / habit / tradition**

Los usos y <u>costumbres</u> de un país reflejan su cultura. ▸ The manners and <u>customs</u> of a country reflect its culture.

creación *n, f* • kɾeaθjOn, kɾeasjOn   **creation**

El autor revela un gran talento en la <u>creación</u> de los personajes. ▸ The author shows a great talent in the <u>creation</u> of his characters.

crear *v* • kɾeaɾ   **to create**

Las religiones asiáticas lo inspiran para <u>crear</u> espléndidas esculturas. ▸ Asian religions inspire him to <u>create</u> splendid sculptures.

creativo/a *adj* • kɾeatiβo   **creative**

Un genio es una persona con un extraordinario talento <u>creativo</u>. ▸ A genius is a person with extraordinary creative abilities.

crítico *n, f/m* • krItiko   **critic**

Ese joven crítico está muy demandado en mucho sitios. ▸ That young critic is in high demand in a lot of places.

cronológico/a *adj* • kronolOxiko   **chronological**

Vamos a describir los acontecimientos en orden cronológico. ▸ Let's describe the events in chronological order.

cuadro *n, m* • kwaðro   **painting**

Picasso pintó este cuadro en 1950. ▸ Picasso painted this picture in 1950.

cubista *adj* • kuβista   **cubist**

¿Podrías nombrar una pintura cubista? ▸ Could you name a cubist painting?

cueva *n, f* • kweβa   **cave**

La cueva es de fácil acceso. ▸ The cave is easy to access.

decoración *n, f* • dekoraθjOn, dekorasjOn   **decoration**

Me encanta la decoración de esta sala. ▸ I love the decoration in this room.

decorar *v* • dekorar   **to decorate**

Gracias por decorar mi casa. ▸ Thank you for decorating my house.

decorativo/a *adj* • dekoratiβo   **decorative / ornamental**

Estoy muy interesada en el arte decorativo. ▸ I'm very interested in decorative art.

democracia *n, f* • demokraθja, demokrasja   **democracy**

La democracia es una idea que se remonta hasta los antiguos griegos. ▸
Democracy is an idea that goes back to the ancient Greeks.

dictadura *n, f* • diktaðura   **dictatorship**

Una dictadura por definición significa un centro de poder. ▸ A dictatorship
means, by definition, one centre of power.

dramaturgo/a *n, f/m* • dramaturɣo   **playwright**

Un estudiante visitó la casa del gran dramaturgo. ▸ A student visited the
house of the great playwright.

edad *n, f* • eðað   **age**

Tienen aproximadamente la misma edad. ▸ They are about the same age.

Edad Contemporánea *n, f* • eðað kontemporAnea   **Modern Age**

¿Cuándo comenzó la Edad Contemporánea? ▸ When did the Modern Age
begin?

Edad Media *n, f* • eðað meðja   **Middle Ages**

La Edad Media comenzó con la caída del Imperio Romano de Occidente. ▸
The Middle Ages began with the fall of the Western Roman Empire.

Edad Moderna *n, f* • eðað moðerna   **Early Modern period**

Estamos estudiando los principales acontecimientos de la Edad Moderna. ▸

We are studying the main events of the Early Modern Period.

emperador *n, m* • emperaðor   **emperor**

El emperador será el símbolo del estado. ▸ The Emperor shall be the symbol of the State.

ensayar *v* • ensajar   **to rehearse / try out**

Vamos a ensayar la cuarta escena. ▸ Let's rehearse the fourth scene.

ensayo *n, m* • ensajo   **essay / rehearsal / trial**

Después de una pausa de diez minutos, continuamos nuestro ensayo. ▸ After a ten-minute break, we resumed our rehearsal.

enterrado *adj* • enteraðo   **buried**

Cristóbal Colón fue enterrado en España. ▸ Christopher Columbus was buried in Spain.

época *n, f* • Epoka   **age / epoch / era / time**

Leyendo libros podemos pasear junto a la gente más importante de cada lugar y cada época. ▸ By reading books we can walk with the great and the good from every place and every era.

escena *n, f* • esθena, essena   **scene**

Esta corta obra de teatro sólo se compone de dos escenas cortas. ▸ This short play is solely made up of two short scenes.

escultor/a *n, f/m* • eskultor   **sculptor**

El escultor dijo que la obra representaba una ventana al cielo. ▸ The sculptor said the work represented a window to the sky.

escultura *n, f* • eskultura   **sculpture**

David tiene un apasionado interés por la escultura. ▸ David has a keen interest in sculpture.

etapa *n, f* • etapa   **stage / phase**

¿Son las naciones la última etapa de la evolución en la sociedad humana? ▸ Are nations the last stage of evolution in human society?

expresar *v* • ekspresar   **to express**

Él sonrió para expresar su consentimiento. ▸ He smiled to express his agreement.

expresivo/a *adj* • ekspresiβo   **expressive**

La música tiene un significado expresivo. ▸ Music has an expressive meaning.

fase *n, f* • fase   **phase / stage**

Se ha completado la primera fase de la construcción. ▸ The first phase of construction has been completed.

folclore *n, m* • folklore   **folklore**

Las sevillanas forman parte del folclore español. ▸ Sevillanas are part of Spanish folklore.

futuro *n, m* • futuro   **future**

Nadie puede decir lo que pasará en el futuro. ▸ No one can tell what'll happen in the <u>future</u>.

genio *n, f/m* • xenjo   **genius**

No hace falta ser un <u>genio</u> para saber quién dijo eso. ▸ You don't have to be a <u>genius</u> to know who said that.

guerra *n, f* • gera   **war**

La <u>guerra</u> es un crimen contra la humanidad. ▸ <u>War</u> is a crime against humanity.

historiador *n, f/m* • istorjaðor   **historian**

Es un <u>historiador</u>. Ahora está estudiando la estructura de la guerra. ▸ He's a <u>historian</u>. He's now studying the structure of war.

histórico/a *adj* • istOriko   **historic / historical**

La novela <u>histórica</u> fue un género muy popular. ▸ The <u>historical</u> novel was a very popular genre.

imagen *n, f* • imaxen   **image / picture**

¿Qué imaginas cuando miras esa <u>imagen</u>? ▸ What do you imagine when you see that <u>picture</u>?

impactar *v* • impaktar   **to affect / to have an impact / to impact**

El terrible suceso <u>impactó</u> a la comunidad. ▸ The terrible event had an <u>impact</u> on the community.

imperial *adj* • imperjal   **imperial**

Los aristócratas vivían al este y al oeste del palacio <u>imperial</u>. ▸ Aristocrats lived to the east and west of the imperial palace.

importancia *n, f* • importanθja, importansja **importance**

Esto es considerado un asunto de gran importancia. ▸ This is considered to be a matter of great importance.

impresionar *v* • impresjonar **to impress**

Lo que más me impresiona de esta pintura es el color. ▸ What impresses me the most about this painting is its color.

impresionismo *n, m* • impresjonizmo **impressionism**

El impresionismo apareció en el siglo XIX. ▸ Impressionism began in the 19th century.

impresionista *adj* • impresjonista **impressionist**

Muchos pintores recibieron la influencia de la escuela impresionista francesa. ▸ Lots of painters were influenced by the French impressionist school.

infinidad *n, f* • imfiniðað **infinity / huge number**

Conocemos una infinidad de lugares históricos. ▸ We know a huge number of historical places.

innegable *adj* • inneɣaβle **undeniable**

La belleza de este cuadro es innegable. ▸ The beauty of this picture is undeniable.

innovar *v* • innoβar **to innovate**

Algunas culturas no permiten que su gente innove. ▸ Some cultures don't allow their people to <u>innovate</u>.

invisible *adj* • imbisiβle   **invisible**

La ignorancia es <u>invisible</u> para aquellos que la sufren. ▸ Ignorance is <u>invisible</u> to those who suffer from it.

lucha *n, f* • luʧa   **battle / fight / struggle**

La historia de su valiente <u>lucha</u> nos conmovió profundamente. ▸ The story of his brave <u>struggle</u> affected us deeply.

madera *n, f* • maðeɾa   **wood**

La mayoría de los templos japoneses están hechos de <u>madera</u>. ▸ The majority of Japanese temples are made out of <u>wood</u>.

marfil *n, m* • maɾfil   **ivory**

Este objeto está hecho de <u>marfil</u>. ▸ This item is made of <u>ivory</u>.

mármol *n, m* • mAɾmol   **marble**

Los pisos de <u>mármol</u> son hermosos. ▸ <u>Marble</u> floors are beautiful.

moderno/a *adj* • moðeɾno   **modern**

Este museo tiene una magnífica colección de arte <u>moderno</u>. ▸ This museum has a magnificent collection of <u>modern</u> art.

monarquía *n, f* • monaɾkIa   **monarchy**

La <u>monarquía</u> francesa parecía invencible; no obstante, fue derribada. ▸ The French <u>monarchy</u> seemed invincible; however, it was overthrown.

movimiento artístico *n, m* • moβimjento aɾtIstiko   **art movement /**

174

artistic movement

El cubismo fue uno de los primeros movimientos artísticos del siglo XX. ▸
Cubism was one of the first art movements of the 20th century.

muralla *n, f* • muraʎa   **wall**

Una muralla rodeaba la vieja ciudad. ▸ A wall surrounded the old city.

música de cámara *n, f* • mUsika de kAmara   **chamber music**

¿Cuándo es el festival de música de cámara? ▸ When's the chamber music
festival?

neolítico/a *adj* • neolItiko   **Neolithic**

El período neolítico también es conocido como la Edad de Piedra Tallada. ▸
The Neolithic period is also known as the Stone Age.

origen *n, m* • orixen   **beginning / descent / origin / spring**

Estaba interesado sobre todo en el origen y desarrollo del universo. ▸ He
was mainly interested in the origin and development of the universe.

original *adj* • orixinal   **original**

¿Es ésta una pieza original? ▸ Is this an original piece?

originalidad *n, f* • orixinaliðað   **originality**

El trabajo que hago ahora requiere de originalidad. ▸ The work I'm doing
now requires originality.

oro *n, m* • oro   **gold**

Numerosos hombres partieron hacia el Oeste en busca de oro. ▸ Many men left for the West in search of gold.

oscuro/a *adj* ● oskuro **dark / gloomy**

El piano está hecho de preciosa madera marrón oscuro. ▸ The piano was made of beautiful, dark brown wood.

paisaje *n, m* ● paisaxe **landscape / scenery**

Cézanne es famoso por sus paisajes. ▸ Cezanne is famous for his landscapes.

paleolítico/a *adj* ● paleolĺtiko **Paleolithic**

Según algunos historiadores, la capacidad del ser humano de dominar el fuego, fue el mayor avance técnico del período paleolítico. ▸ According to some historians, the ability of human beings to master fire was the greatest technological advance of the Palaeolithic period.

parlamento *n, m* ● parlamento **parliament**

El parlamento tuvo su origen en la Inglaterra del siglo XIV. ▸ Parliament has its beginnings in 14th-century England.

pasado *n, m* ● pasaðo **past**

Si no fuera por los libros, cada generación tendría que redescubrir por sí misma las verdades del pasado. ▸ If it were not for books, each generation would have to rediscover for itself the truths of the past.

período *n, m* ● perĺoðo **era / period / season**

Muchos han sufrido la opresión y la miseria durante un largo período de tiempo bajo el dominio del colonialismo. ▸ Many have suffered oppression and misery for a long period of time under the rule of colonialism.

pintor *n, f/m* • pintor **painter**

Él es un pintor famoso y debería de ser tratado como tal. ▸ He is a famous painter and should be treated as such.

pintura *n, f* • pintura **paint / painting**

Esta es una foto de mi pintura. ▸ This is a picture of my own painting.

plata *n, f* • plata **silver**

¿Sabes cuál es la diferencia entre plata y estaño? ▸ Do you know the difference between silver and tin?

poesía *n, f* • poesIa **poetry**

Ya se ha dicho mucho acerca de la dificultad de traducir poesía. ▸ Much has already been said about the difficulty of translating poetry.

poeta *n, f/m* • poeta **poet**

Ella no es poeta, es novelista. ▸ She is not a poet but a novelist.

poético/a *adj* • poEtiko **poetic**

Me encanta el estilo poético de Lorca. ▸ I love Lorca's poetic style.

polémica *n, f* • polEmika **controversy / polemic**

La decisión del partido marcó el principio de las controversias. ▸ The party's decision marked the beginning of controversies.

prehistoria *n, f* • preistorja **prehistory**

Aprender sobre la prehistoria es fascinante. ▸ Learning about prehistory is fascinating.

prehistórico/a adj • preistOriko   **prehistoric**

Estoy leyendo un libro sobre arqueología prehistórica. ▸ I'm reading a book on prehistoric archeology.

primitivo/a adj • primitiβo   **primitive**

Vamos a ver una exposición de herramientas primitivas. ▸ We're going to an exhibition of primitive tools.

producir v • proðuθir, proðusir   **to make / to produce**

Ellos sabían como producir hierro. ▸ They knew how to make iron.

productivo/a adj • proðuktiβo   **productive**

El autor tiene setenta años, pero no es menos productivo que cuando tenía veinte años menos. ▸ The author is seventy, but he's no less productive than he was twenty years ago.

puente n, m • pwente   **bridge**

Varios puentes han sido dañados o destruidos. ▸ Several bridges have been damaged or swept away.

realista adj • realista   **realist / realistic / royalist**

Es un plan realista. ▸ It's a realistic plan.

recinto n, m • reθinto, resinto   **enclosure / facility / precinct**

Aquí podemos ver la entrada al recinto amurallado. ▸ Here we can see the entrance to the walled enclosure.

reconocible *adj* • rekonoθiβle, rekonosiβle **recognizable**

Sus pinturas son claramente reconocibles. ▸ Her paintings are clearly recognizable.

representante *n, f/m* • representante **representative**

Toda persona tiene derecho a participar en el gobierno de su país, directamente o por medio de representantes libremente escogidos. ▸ Everyone has the right to take part in the government of his country, directly or through freely chosen representatives.

representar *v* • representar **to depict / to represent**

¿Qué representa el color negro en este cuadro? ▸ What does the black color represent in this picture?

rima *n, f* • rima **rhyme**

Este poema tiene rima asonante. ▸ This poem has assonant rhyme.

sinagoga *n, f* • sinaɣoɣa **synagogue**

Cerca de la plaza del mercado hay una imponente sinagoga. ▸ Near the market square there is an imposing synagogue.

surrealismo *n, m* • surealizmo **surrealism**

Este libro está lleno de misterio y surrealismo. ▸ This book is full of mystery and surrealism.

surrealista *adj* • surealista **surrealist / surreal**

Mi madre es una amante del arte surrealista. ▸ My mum is a surreal art lover.

talento *n, m* • talento
gift / skill / talent

Siento admiración por su talento. ▸ I feel admiration for his talent.

teatral *adj* • teatral
theater / theatrical

Voy a unirme a una compañía teatral. ▸ I'm joining a theater company.

técnica *n, f* • tEknika
technique

Su técnica fue única y totalmente asombrosa. ▸ His technique was unique and absolutely amazing.

teoría *n, f* • teoɾla
theory

Su teoría merece consideración. ▸ His theory deserves consideration.

torre *n, f* • tore
tower

La Torre Eiffel es más alta que las torres de la Catedral de Colonia. ▸ The Eiffel Tower is taller than the towers of the Cologne Cathedral.

vanguardia *n, f* • baŋgwarðja
avant-garde / forefront / vanguard

Hoy analizaremos algunos pintores de vanguardia. ▸ Today we're analyzing some avant-garde painters.

vanguardismo *n, m* • baŋgwarðizmo
avant-garde movement / vanguardism

¿Cuál es la principall característica del vanguardismo? ▸ What's the main feature of the avant-garde movement?

vanguardista *adj* • baŋgwarðista
avant-garde

El cubismo es un movimiento <u>vanguardista</u>. ▸ Cubism is an <u>avant-garde</u> movement.

verso *n, m* • berso   **line / verse**

No puedo recordar cómo empieza el segundo <u>verso</u>. ▸ I can't remember how the second <u>verse</u> starts.

visible *adj* • bisiβle   **apparent / visible**

El autor está presente en todas partes y en ninguna parte <u>visible</u>. ▸ The author is present everywhere and <u>visible</u> nowhere.

9 Media & Communication

acceder *v* • akθeðeɾ, akseðeɾ   **to accede / (have) access**

¿Cómo puedo acceder a la impresora? ▸ How can I access the printer?

accesible *adj* • akθesiβle, aksesiβle   **accessible / approachable**

¿Cuándo se hizo el teléfono móvil accesible para todos? ▸ When did the mobile phone become accessible to all?

acceso *n, m* • akθeso, akseso   **access / entry**

¡Consigue teléfono y acceso a internet en un solo paquete! ▸ Get both a phone and internet access in a single package!

actual *adj* • aktwal   **current / ongoing / present**

Él consiguió su actual posición en virtud de su larga experiencia. ▸ He got his present position by virtue of his long experience.

actualidad *n, f* • aktwaliðað   **current affairs / news**

¿Qué sabes de la actualidad política española? ▸ What do you know about political news in Spain?

actualizar *v* • aktwaliθaɾ, aktwalisaɾ   **to update**

¿Me podrías actualizar estos datos? ▸ Could I get you to update this data for me?

actualmente *adv* • aktwalmente   **currently / nowadays / today**

Este plan actualmente se encuentra bajo consideración. ‣ This plan is currently under consideration.

acuerdo *n, m* • akwerðo   **agreement / arrangement / deal**

Necesitamos llegar a un acuerdo. ‣ We need to come to an agreement.

adjuntar *v* • aðxuntar   **to attach**

He adjuntado el documento. ‣ I have attached the document.

ambiente *n, m* • ambjente   **ambiance / atmosphere / environment**

La destrucción de la capa de ozono afecta al medio ambiente. ‣ The destruction of the ozone layer affects the environment.

ámbito *n, m* • Ambito   **field**

Como traductora, estoy especializada en dos campos. ‣ As a translator, I'm specialized in two fields.

animar *v* • animar   **to cheer up / to encourage**

Tenemos que animar a la gente a unirse a la campaña y a trabajar con nosotros. ‣ We have to encourage people to join the campaign and work with us.

anormal *adj* • anormal   **aberrant / abnormal**

¿Qué conclusión sacas de su comportamiento anormal? ‣ What do you conclude from her abnormal behavior?

anunciar *v* • anunθjar, anunsjar   **to advertise / to announce**

Tengo que <u>anunciar</u> algo importante. ▸ I have something important to <u>announce</u>.

archivo *n, m* • arʧiβo **dossier / file**

¿Cuál es el <u>archivo</u> correcto? ▸ Which one is the correct <u>file</u>?

atmósfera *n, f* • atmOsfera **ambiance / atmosphere**

Este lugar tiene una <u>atmósfera</u> misteriosa. ▸ This place has a mysterious <u>atmosphere</u>.

batería *n, f* • baterIa **battery**

Debería haber dejado cargando la <u>batería</u> de la cámara. ▸ I should have left the camera <u>battery</u> recharging.

blog *n, m* • bloɣ **blog**

¿Acerca de qué es tu <u>blog</u>? ▸ What's your <u>blog</u> about?

breve *adj* • breβe **short / brief**

Me gustan los poemas <u>breves</u>. ▸ I like <u>short</u> poems.

buscador *n, m* • buskaðoɾ **searcher / browser**

Primero tienes que abrir el <u>buscador</u>. ▸ First you have to start up the <u>browser</u>.

cable *n, m* • kaβle **cable**

Necesito un <u>cable</u> USB nuevo. ▸ I need a new USB <u>cable</u>.

canal *n, m* • kanal **channel**

Me gustaría poner el <u>canal</u> de las películas. ▸ I'd like to set it to the movie <u>channel</u>.

cargador *n, m* • karɣaðoɾ   **charger**

¿Has visto el <u>cargador</u> de mi teléfono? ▸ Have you seen my phone <u>charger</u>?

cargar *v* • karɣaɾ   **to carry / to charge / to load**

Necesito <u>cargar</u> mi móvil. ▸ I need to <u>charge</u> my mobile.

carta *n, f* • kaɾta   **card / letter / menu**

No olvides pegar el sello a la <u>carta</u>. ▸ Don't forget to put a stamp on your <u>letter</u>.

cartelera *n, f* • kaɾtelera   **billboard / entertainment page**

¿Hay algo interesante en la <u>cartelera</u>? ▸ Is there anything interesting in the <u>entertainment</u> page?

celular *adj* • θelulaɾ, selulaɾ   **cell / mobile**

La invención del <u>celular</u> tuvo lugar en los años setenta y se hizo accesible para todos en los años ochenta y noventa. ▸ The invention of the <u>mobile</u> phone took place in the seventies, and it became accessible to all in the eighties and nineties.

cerrar sesión *v* • seraɾ sesjOn   **to log out**

No olvides <u>cerrar sesión</u> cuando termines. ▸ Don't forget to <u>log out</u> when you finish.

chatear *v* • ʧateaɾ   **to chat**

Ya que estoy aquí, ¿te gustaría chatear? ▸ Since I'm here, would you like to chat?

ciencias de la información *n, f* • sjensjas de la imformasjOn **information science**

Mi hermana tiene un grado en ciencias de la información. ▸ My sister has a degree in information science.

cobertura *n, f* • koβertura   **coverage / hedge / reception**

La cobertura mediática es clave en las campañas políticas. ▸ Media coverage is key in political campaigns.

código *n, m* • kOðiɣo   **code**

Todos los empleados tuvieron que memorizar el código de acceso. ▸ All employees had to memorize the access code.

coger el teléfono *v* • koxer el telEfono   **to answer the phone**

No coge el teléfono porque está dormida. ▸ She doesn't answer the phone because she is asleep.

colgar el teléfono *v* • kolgar el telEfono   **to hang up**

Si no cuelgas el teléfono, no podré usarlo. ▸ If you don't hang up, I won't be able to use the phone.

computador *n, m* • komputaðor   **computer**

Su computador se reiniciará varias veces durante la instalación. ▸ Your computer will restart several times during installation.

comunicación *n, f* • komunikaθjOn, komunikasjOn   **communication**

187

Debido a los modernos sistemas de comunicación y transporte, el mundo se está volviendo pequeño. ▸ Because of modern communication and transportation systems, the world is getting smaller.

comunicar *v* • komunikar   **to communicate**

Nos podemos comunicar en francés. ▸ We can communicate in French.

conectado/a *adj* • konektaðo   **connected / on-line**

Solo he estado conectado durante diez minutos. ▸ I've only been online for ten minutes.

conectar *v* • konektar   **to connect**

Su trabajo es conectar los computadores a la red. ▸ Their job is to connect the computers to the network.

conectarse *v* • konektarse   **to go online**

Me conecto a internet cada mañana. ▸ I go online every morning.

conexión *n, f* • koneksjOn   **connection**

Me cortaron la conexión a Internet. ▸ My internet connection was cut off.

confiar *v* • komfjar   **to trust**

No sé hasta qué punto puedo confiar en ellos. ▸ I have no idea to what extent I can trust them.

conocido/a *adj* • konoθiðo, konosiðo   **acquaintance / well-known**

Mahjong es un juego muy conocido en el mundo. ▸ Mahjong is a game well-known all around the world.

consultar *v* • konsultar **to consult / to look up**

Mejor consultar un diccionario cuando no sabes el significado de una palabra. ▸ You had better consult a dictionary when you don't know the meaning of a word.

contenido *n, m* • konteniðo **contents**

El contenido de la carta era secreto. ▸ The contents of the letter were secret.

contestación *n, f* • kontestaθjo, kontestasjon **answer**

Todavía no hemos recibido ninguna contestación. ▸ We haven't received any answer yet.

contraseña *n, f* • kontraseɲa **password**

La contraseña que ha introducido no es válida. ▸ The password you have entered is invalid.

copia *n, f* • kopja **copy**

Le daré una copia a cualquiera que la pida. ▸ I'll give a copy to anyone who asks for it.

correo *n, m* • koreo **mail**

¿Hay correo hoy? ▸ Did the mail come today?

creíble *adj* • kreIβle **believable / credible / likely**

Eso es difícilmente creíble. ▸ That's hardly believable.

cuenta *n, f* • kwenta **account**

¿Tienes cuenta en alguna página de redes sociales? ▸ Do you have an account with any social networking web sites?

datos *n, m* • datos **data**

Los datos no han sido compilados aún. ▸ The data hasn't been compiled yet.

datos móviles *n, m* • datos mOβiles **mobile data**

Aquí es necesario pasar del wifi a los datos móviles. ▸ Here it's necessary to switch from wifi to mobile data.

debate *n, m* • deβate **debate**

Preferiría quedarme fuera de ese debate porque no quiero problemas. ▸ I'd better stay out of that debate as I don't want any trouble.

debatir *v* • deβatir **to argue / to debate**

Yo solía debatir el problema con ella. ▸ I used to debate the problem with her.

desacuerdo *n, m* • desakwerðo **disagreement**

Nosotros teníamos un pequeño desacuerdo acerca de eso. ▸ We had quite a disagreement about it.

descargar *v* • deskarɣar **to download / to unload**

Puedes descargar grabaciones de nativos en nuestra página web. ▸ You can download audio files by native speakers from our website.

desconectar *v* • deskonektar   **to disconnect / go offline**

¿Por qué te desconectaste tan pronto? ▸ Why did you go offline so early?

desconexión *n, f* • deskoneksjOn   **disconnection**

¿Qué causó la desconexión entre los dispositivos? ▸ What caused the disconnection between the devices?

desconfiar *v* • deskomfjar   **to distrust / to mistrust**

Deberías desconfiar de esta información. ▸ You should distrust this information.

desconocido/a *adj* • deskonoθiðo, deskonosiðo   **stranger / unknown**

Aunque la mayoría de las islas en el océano han sido mapeadas, el suelo oceánico es por lo general desconocido. ▸ Although most islands in the ocean have been mapped, the ocean floor is generally unknown.

desinformado/a *adj* • desimformaðo   **uninformed**

Si no lees los diarios, estás desinformado. ▸ If you don't read the newspapers, you're uninformed.

diferenciar *v* • diferenθjar, diferensjar   **to differentiate**

No podía diferenciarme de los otros candidatos. ▸ I couldn't differentiate myself from the other candidates.

difusión *n, f* • difusjOn   **dissemination / broadcasting / spreading / diffusion**

Sin la difusión de los hechos, las teorías conspirativas abundarán. ▸ Without dissemination of the facts, conspiracy theories will abound.

discriminación *n, f* • diskriminaθjOn, diskriminasjOn   **bigotry /
discrimination**

La multitud protestó contra la discriminación racial. ▸ The crowd protested
against racial discrimination.

discriminar *v* • diskriminar   **to discriminate**

En esta empresa, no discriminamos a nadie. ▸ In this company, we never
discriminate against anybody.

discriminatorio/a *adj* • diskriminatorjo   **discriminatory**

Ninguna práctica discriminatoria será aceptada en esta comunidad. ▸ No
discriminatory practice will be accepted in this community.

edición *n, f* • eðiθjOn, eðisjOn   **edition**

Que yo sepa, es la edición más reciente. ▸ As far as I know, this is the latest
edition.

editar *v* • eðitar   **to edit**

Para editar una frase, haga clic en el icono de lápiz. ▸ To edit a sentence,
click on the pencil icon.

editorial *n, f* • eðitorjal   **editorial / publisher / publishing house**

Esa editorial está especializada en literatura infantil. ▸ That publisher spe-
cialises in children's books.

eliminación *n, f* • eliminaθjOn, eliminasjOn   **elimination / removal**

Lucharon por la eliminación de la homofobia. ▸ They fought for the elimination of homophobia.

enchufe *n, m* • eɳʧufe   **plug / socket**

Necesito el alargador, el enchufe está demasiado lejos. ▸ I need the extension cord. The socket is too far.

encuesta *n, f* • eɳkwesta   **poll / survey**

Una encuesta muestra que una gran mayoría está a favor de la legislación.
▸ A poll shows that an overwhelming majority is in favor of the legislation.

entretener *v* • entretener   **to amuse / to entertain**

¿Cómo os entretenéis los fines de semana? ▸ How do you entertain yourselves on the weekends?

entretenido/a *adj* • entreteniðo   **amusing / enjoyable / entertaining**

Fue interesante y entretenido. ▸ It was interesting and amusing.

entretenimiento *n, m* • entretenimjento   **entertainment**

El fin último de todas las artes no es otro que el entretenimiento. ▸ All arts' aim is no other than entertainment.

entrevista *n, f* • entreβista   **interview**

¿Cómo te fue en la entrevista? ▸ How did your interview go?

entrevistar *v* • entreβistar   **to interview**

¿A quién querrías entrevistar? ▸ Who would you like to interview?

esencial *adj* • esenθjal, esensjal   **essential**

Para mi la cámara fue <u>esencial</u>. ▸ The camera was <u>essential</u> for me.

especializado/a *adj* • espeθjaliθaðo, espesjalisaðo   **specialized**

No puedo entender el texto por su vocabulario tan <u>especializado</u>. ▸ I cannot understand the text because of its <u>specialized</u> vocabulary.

establecer *v* • estaβleθer, estaβleser   **to ascertain / to establish**

Nuestra meta final es <u>establecer</u> la paz mundial. ▸ Our ultimate goal is to <u>establish</u> world peace.

estar al día *v* • estar al día   **to be up to date**

¿<u>Estás al día</u> de las nuevas tecnologías? ▸ <u>Are</u> you <u>up to date</u> with new technologies?

existencia *n, f* • eksistenθja, eksistensja   **existence**

La <u>existencia</u> determina la conciencia. ▸ <u>Existence</u> determines conscience.

existente *adj* • eksistente   **actual / existent / existing**

Todo lo que consideramos <u>existente</u> presupone la conciencia. ▸ Everything that we regard as <u>existing</u>, postulates consciousness.

existir *v* • eksistir   **to exist**

Ninguna nación puede <u>existir</u> completamente aislada de otras. ▸ No nation can <u>exist</u> completely isolated from others.

fiable *adj* • fjaβle   **reliable / trustworthy**

El pronóstico del tiempo no es necesariamente <u>fiable</u>. ▸ The weather forecast is not necessarily reliable.

formulario *n, m* • formularjo   **form**

Por favor rellene este formulario. ▸ Please fill out this form.

gráfico *n, m / adj* • grAfiko   **graph / graphic**

No entiendo este gráfico. ▸ I don't understand this graph.

identidad *n, f* • iðentiðað   **identity**

El criminal tuvo que ocultar su identidad. ▸ The criminal had to conceal his identity.

impacto *n, m* • impakto   **impact**

El impacto de la ciencia en la sociedad es grande. ▸ The impact of science on society is great.

inalámbrico/a *adj* • inalAmbriko   **wireless**

Ayer compré un micrófono inalámbrico para mi trabajo. ▸ Yesterday I bought a wireless microphone for my work.

indicar *v* • indikar   **to indicate / to point / to state**

En español hay muchas expresiones diferentes para indicar cambios y transformaciones. ▸ In Spanish, there are many different expressions to indicate changes and transformations.

información *n, f* • imformaθjOn, imformasjOn   **information**

Tenemos la información equivocada. ▸ We have the wrong information.

informado/a *adj* • imformaðo   **informed**

Tratamos de mantenernos informadas. ► We try to stay informed.

informática *n, f* • imformAtika   **computing / IT**

La informática es su pasión. ► Computing is his passion.

informativo/a *adj* • imformatiβo   **informative**

Este manual es puramente informativo. ► This manual is mainly informative.

iniciar *v* • iniθjar, inisjar   **to begin / to start / to log in**

Vamos a iniciar una investigación contra él. ► We are going to start a research on him.

inicio de sesión *n, m* • inisjo de sesjOn   **log in / log on**

Necesitas la contraseña para el inicio de sesión. ► You need the password to log in.

innecesario/a *adj* • inneθesarjo, innesesarjo   **pointless / unnecessary**

Pensé que era innecesario que hiciéramos algo al respecto hoy. ► I thought it was unnecessary for us to do anything about that today.

insignificante *adj* • insiɣnifikante   **insignificant**

Aunque pienses que es insignificante, hacerlo te ayudará. ► Even though you might think it's insignificant, doing it will help you.

instalar *v* • instalar   **to install**

Intenté instalar un nuevo navegador. ► I tried to install a new browser.

intento *n, m* • intento   **attempt / go / try**

Él fracasó en su intento de atravesar el río a nado. ▸ He failed in his attempt to swim across the river.

línea fija *n, f* • lInea fixa **landline**

No tenemos línea fija desde hace dos años. ▸ We haven't had a landline for the last two years.

llamada *n, f* • ʎamaða **call**

Quisiera hacer una llamada telefónica. ▸ I would like to make a phone call.

mensajear *v* • mensaxeaɾ **to message / to text**

Mensajéame cuando tengas tiempo. ▸ Text me when you have the time.

mensajería instantánea *n, f* • mensaxeɾIa instantAnea **instant messaging**

La mensajería instantánea es una forma rápida y práctica de comunicación. ▸ Instant messaging is a fast and practical way of communication.

nacional *adj* • naθjonal, nasjonal **national**

Cada país tiene su bandera nacional. ▸ Every country has its national flag.

noticia *n, f* • notiθja, notisja **news**

¿Tienes alguna buena noticia? ▸ Do you have any good news?

noticia bomba *n, f* • notisja bomba **bombshell**

Creo que esto es una noticia bomba. ▸ I believe this news is a bombshell.

noticia falsa *n, f* • notisja falsa **fake news**

Hoy en día las noticias falsas se difunden con rapidez. ▸ Nowadays fake news spread fast.

noticiario *n, m* • notiθjarjo, notisjarjo   **news broadcast**

Este noticiario es fiable. ▸ This news broadcast is reliable.

novedad *n, f* • noβeðað   **newness / novelty**

Este producto es una novedad interesantísima. ▸ This product is an interesting novelty.

novedoso/a *adj* • noβeðoso   **novel**

Este misterio tiene un vuelco en la trama completamente novedoso. ▸ This mystery has a plot twist that's completely novel.

opinar *v* • opinar   **to believe / to think / to give your opinion**

¿Qué opinas sobre todo esto? ▸ What do you think about all this?

opinión *n, f* • opinjOn   **opinion**

No soy el único que tiene esta opinión. ▸ I am not alone in this opinion.

oyente *n, f/m* • ojente   **listener**

Los oyentes de este programa son en general muy jóvenes. ▸ Listeners of this program are generally quite young.

pantalla *n, f* • pantaʎa   **screen**

Este teléfono tiene una pantalla multitáctil. ▸ This phone has a multitouch screen.

participación *n, f* • partiθipaθjOn, partisipasjOn   **participation / share /**

stake

La participación es voluntaria y gratuita. ▸ Participation is voluntary and free of charge.

periódico *n, m* • perjoðiko   **newspaper**

Debes leer el periódico para poder seguir el ritmo de los tiempos. ▸ You must read the newspaper so that you may keep up with the times.

periodismo *n, m* • perjoðizmo   **journalism**

En una democracia, es importante que el periodismo sea independiente. ▸ In a democracy, it is important for journalism to be independent.

pluralidad *n, f* • pluraliðað   **diversity / variety**

La pluralidad de opiniones en política es simplemente natural. ▸ Diversity of opinions in politics is simply natural.

pluralismo *n, m* • pluralizmo   **pluralism**

La diversidad cultural y el pluralismo son elementos importantes en una sociedad moderna. ▸ Cultural diversity and pluralism are important elements of modern societies.

población *n, f* • poβlaθjOn, poβlasjOn   **population**

¿Cuál es la población total de Francia? ▸ What's the total population of France?

poder *n, m* • poðer   **power**

El poder conlleva responsabilidades. ▸ Power entails responsibilities.

postura *n, f* • postura   **position / posture**

Él está reconsiderando sus <u>posturas</u> acerca de la política actual. ▸ He is reconsidering his <u>positions</u> on current politics.

prensa *n, f* • prensa   **press**

La conferencia de <u>prensa</u> está agendada para dar comienzo dentro de una hora. ▸ The <u>press</u> conference is scheduled to begin one hour from now.

privado/a *adj* • priβaðo   **private**

Me lo contó en <u>privado</u>. ▸ He told me about it in <u>private</u>.

programación *n, f* • proɣramaθjOn, proɣramasjOn   **programming**

Estamos aprendiendo <u>programación</u>. ▸ We are learning <u>programming</u>.

promover *v* • promoβer   **to encourage / to promote**

El gobierno debería <u>promover</u> el bienestar común. ▸ The government should <u>promote</u> common welfare.

proveedor *n, m* • proβeeðor   **provider / supplier**

Estoy pensando en cambiar de <u>proveedor</u>. ▸ I'm thinking about changing my <u>supplier</u>.

público *n, m* • pUβliko   **audience / public**

Nuestras encuestas indican que el <u>público</u> apoyaría la legislación propuesta. ▸ Our surveys indicate that the <u>public</u> would support the proposed legislation.

radiofónico/a *adj* • raðjofOniko   **radio broadcasting**

Este programa <u>radiofónico</u> es increíblemente popular. ▸ This <u>radio</u> program is incredibly popular.

reciente *adj* • reθjente, resjente   **recent**

Adjunte una fotografía <u>reciente</u> a su formulario de solicitud. ▸ Attach a <u>recent</u> photograph to your application form.

red *n, f* • reð   **net / network**

Reparó la <u>red</u>. ▸ He fixed the <u>net</u>.

reenviar *v* • reembjar   **to forward**

¿Podrías <u>reenviar</u> el e-mail a todos los empleados? ▸ Could you <u>forward</u> the e-mail to all the employees?

registrarse *v* • rexistrarse   **to register**

Tiene que <u>registrarse</u> antes de realizar la compra. ▸ You have to <u>register</u> before putting your purchase through.

regular *v* • reɣular   **to regulate / to standardize**

Los semáforos se usan para <u>regular</u> el tráfico. ▸ Traffic lights are used to <u>regulate</u> traffic.

renovar *v* • renoβar   **to renew / to renovate**

Necesito <u>renovar</u> mi suscripción. ▸ I need to <u>renew</u> my subscription.

revista *n, f* • reβista   **magazine**

¿Cuántos suscriptores tiene esta <u>revista</u>? ▸ How many subscribers does this <u>magazine</u> have?

sección *n, f* • sekθjOn, seksjOn   **section**

Lea la sección de anuncios si busca empleo. ▸ Read the advertisement section if you're looking for a job.

soporte *n, m* • soporte **base / format / foundation / support**

Les ofrecemos soporte técnico gratuito. ▸ We offer you free technical support.

suscripción *n, f* • suskripθjOn, suskripsjOn **subscription**

Necesito renovar mi suscripción. ▸ I need to renew my subscription.

suscriptor/a *n, f/m* • suskriptor **subscriber**

Soy suscriptor de un periódico semanal. ▸ I'm a subscriber for a weekly journal.

tarifa plana *n, f* • tarifa plana **flat rate**

La mayoría de la gente que conozco elige pagar una tarifa plana de internet. ▸ Most people I know prefer to pay a flat rate for the internet.

tarjeta *n, f* • tarxeta **card**

Él le mandó una tarjeta a Mary. ▸ He sent a card to Mary.

teclado *n, m* • teklaðo **keyboard**

Este teclado es perfecto. ▸ This keyboard is perfect.

telediario *n, m* • teleðjarjo **TV news**

Laura está viendo el telediario. ▸ Laura is watching the news on television.

telefonear *v* • telefonear **to call / to phone / to ring**

Justo cuando le iba a <u>telefonear</u>, llegó una carta de ella. ▸ Just when I was about to <u>phone</u> her, a letter arrived from her.

telefonía móvil *n, f* • telefonIa mOβil   **cell phone / mobile phone**

La <u>telefonía móvil</u> ha cambiado mucho en los últimos 20 años. ▸ The <u>mobile phone</u> has changed so much in the last 20 years.

telefónico/a *adj* • telefOniko   **telephone**

Se me olvida tu número <u>telefónico</u>. ▸ I forget your <u>telephone</u> number.

teléfono móvil *n, m* • telEfono mOβil   **cell / mobile**

Conozco a dos personas que no tienen <u>teléfono móvil</u>. ▸ I know two people who don't have a <u>mobile</u>.

tema *n, m* • tema   **matter / subject / topic**

Ella cambió de <u>tema</u>. ▸ She changed the <u>subject</u>.

titulares *n, m* • titulares   **headlines**

Mi madre echó una ojeada a los <u>titulares</u>. ▸ My mother glanced at the <u>headlines</u>.

usuario/a *n, f/m* • uswarjo   **user**

¿Te gustaría convertirte en <u>usuario</u> de confianza? ▸ Would you like to become a trusted <u>user</u>?

10 Means of Transport

acampar *v* • akampaɾ **to camp**

Mucha gente está interesada en <u>acampar</u>. ▸ A lot of people are interested in <u>camping</u>.

acercarse *v* • aθerkarse, aserkarse **to approach / move closer**

¿Puede <u>acercarse</u> hacia mí? ▸ Can you <u>move closer</u> to me?

acompañar *v* • akompaɲaɾ **to accompany / go with**

Voy a <u>acompañarte</u>. ▸ I'll <u>go with</u> you.

aéreo/a *adj* • aEɾeO **air / aerial**

El paquete fue enviado por vía <u>aérea</u>. ▸ The parcel was sent by <u>air</u>.

agencia *n, f* • axenθja, axensja **agency**

Trabajo en una <u>agencia</u> de viajes. ▸ I work in a travel <u>agency</u>.

alejarse *v* • alexarse **to distance / get away / move away**

Nos <u>alejamos</u> de la multitud. ▸ We <u>moved away</u> from the crowd.

alojamiento *n, m* • aloxamjento **accommodation / housing / lodging**

La aerolínea ofreció <u>alojamiento</u> gratuito a los pasajeros atrapados como un gesto de buena voluntad. ► The airline provided free <u>accommodation</u> to stranded passengers as a goodwill gesture.

alojarse *v* • aloxarse   **to stay**

¿Cuánta gente se <u>alojó</u> en tu casa? ► How many people <u>stayed</u> at your place?

andén *n, m* • andEn   **platform**

El tren hacia Birmingham sale del <u>andén</u> 3. ► The train for Birmingham leaves from <u>platform</u> 3.

área *n, f* • Area   **area**

El <u>área</u> residencial es agradable para vivir en ella. ► This residential <u>area</u> is comfortable to live in.

área de descanso *n, f* • Area de deskanso   **rest area**

Vamos a parar un momento en el <u>área de descanso</u>. ► We're going to stop for a while in the <u>rest area</u>.

atasco *n, m* • atasko   **congestion / traffic jam**

El autobús llegó tarde por el <u>atasco</u>. ► The bus was late because of the <u>traffic jam</u>.

atravesar *v* • atraβesar   **to cross / to go through**

Ella pudo <u>atravesar</u> el océano Pacífico en bote. ► She was able to <u>cross</u> the Pacific Ocean by boat.

aventura *n, f* • aβentura   **adventure**

Él sintió el aliciente de la aventura. ▸ He felt the lure of adventure.

aventurarse *v* • aβenturarse **to venture**

¿Por qué te aventuraste en una zona desconocida? ▸ Why did you venture into an unknown area?

barca *n, f* • barka **boat**

La barca se hundió hasta el fondo del lago. ▸ The boat sank to the bottom of the lake.

bienvenida *n, f* • bjembeniða **welcome**

Hubo una fiesta de bienvenida en el restaurante. ▸ A welcome party took place in the restaurant.

billete *n, m* • biʎete **ticket**

Habríamos comprado los billetes de avión si el precio hubiese sido un poco más bajo. ▸ We would have bought the plane tickets if the price had been a little lower.

cámara *n, f* • kAmara **camera**

Me gustaría comprar una cámara como esta. ▸ I would like to get a camera like this.

campamento *n, m* • kampamento **camp / campsite / encampment**

Me gustaría apuntarme al campamento de verano. ▸ I would like to join the summer camp.

camping *n, m* • kampiŋ **camping / campsite**

Ellos se van de camping todos los veranos. ▸ They go camping every summer.

cancelar *v* • kanθelaɾ, kanselaɾ   **to call off / to cancel**

Tenemos que cancelar nuestro viaje a Japón. ‣ We must cancel our trip to Japan.

carretera *n, f* • kaɾeteɾa   **highway / road**

La carretera se curva hacia la derecha en este punto. ‣ The road bends sharply to the right at this point.

cercanía *n, f* • θeɾkanIa, seɾkanIa   **proximity**

Siento la cercanía de las vacaciones. ‣ I feel the proximity of the holidays.

cercano/a *adj* • θeɾkano, seɾkano   **close / nearby**

Ellos caminaron con él hasta un edificio de madera cercano a la granja. ‣ They walked with him to an old wooden building near the farmhouse.

circulación *n, f* • θiɾkulaθjOn, siɾkulasjOn   **circulation / traffic**

No conozco el reglamento de la circulación aquí. ‣ I don't know the traffic regulations here.

clase turista *n, f* • klase tuɾista   **economy class**

Sí, siempre viajamos en clase turista. ‣ Yes, we always travel in economy class.

comodidad *n, f* • komoðiðað   **amenity / comfort / convenience**

Se puso poca atención en la comodidad de los pasajeros. ‣ Little attention was paid to the comfort for the passengers.

cómodo/a *adj* • kOmoðo   **comfortable / convenient**

Este tren es cómodo. ▸ This train is comfortable.

compañía *n, f* • kompaɲIa   **company**

En esta compañía, debes ser capaz de hablar inglés o español. ▸ You must be able to speak either English or Spanish in this company.

conducción *n, f* • kondukθjOn, konduksjOn   **driving**

Muéstreme su permiso de conducción, por favor. ▸ Show me your driving license, please.

conducir *v* • konduθir, kondusir   **to drive**

La próxima vez me toca conducir. ▸ Next time it will be my turn to drive.

conexión *n, f* • koneksjOn   **connection**

La conexión más rápida es a través de Roma. ▸ The fastest connection is through Rome.

contratar un viaje *v* • kontratar un bjaxe   **to book a trip**

Ya hemos contratado nuestro próximo viaje. ▸ We've already booked our next trip.

crucero *n, m* • kruθero, krusero   **cruise**

He utilizado recientemente los servicios de su agencia de viajes para contratar un crucero por el Mediterráneo. ▸ I have recently used the services of his travel agency to book a cruise in the Mediterranean.

decanso *n, m* • dekanso   **break / rest**

Vamos a tomarnos un descanso de 5 minutos. ▸ Let's take a 5 minutes break.

descansar *v* • deskansar   **to rest / to have a break**

Después de tantas visitas queremos descansar un poco. ▸ After so many visits, we want to rest a little.

despedida *n, f* • despeðiða   **farewell / good-bye**

Mañana le haremos una reunión de despedida a Nancy. ▸ Tomorrow, we're holding a farewell gathering for Nancy.

despedirse *v* • despeðirse   **to bid farewell / say goodbye / see off**

Aunque estaba muy ocupada, vino a despedirse de mí. ▸ Though very busy, she came to see me off.

destino *n, m* • destino   **destination / destiny**

Por fin llegamos a nuestro destino. ▸ At last, we reached our destination.

destino turístico *n, m* • destino turIstiko   **tourist destination**

¿Tienes un destino turístico preferido? ▸ Do you have a favorite tourist destination?

documentación *n, f* • dokumentaθjOn, dokumentasjOn **documentation / identification**

Debes mostrar tu documentación en la entrada. ▸ You must show your iden-

<u>tification</u> at the entrance.

embarcar *v* • embarkar   **to board / embark**

Estamos a punto de <u>embarcar</u> en el avión. ▸ We're about to <u>board</u> the plane.

embarque *n, m* • embarke   **boarding**

¿Dónde está la puerta de <u>embarque</u>? ▸ Where is the <u>boarding</u> gate?

embotellamiento *n, m* • emboteʎamjento   **traffic jam**

Quedé atrapado en un <u>embotellamiento</u>. ▸ I was caught in a <u>traffic jam</u>.

encontrarse *v* • eŋkontrarse   **to be / find yourself / meet**

Me <u>encuentro</u> solo en mi casa. ▸ I <u>am</u> alone at home.

encuentro *n, m* • eŋkwentro   **meeting**

Alicia no estuvo presente en el <u>encuentro</u>, ¿no es así? ▸ Alice wasn't present at the <u>meeting</u>, was she?

equipaje *n, m* • ekipaxe   **baggage / luggage**

Tengo el <u>equipaje</u> en el maletero. ▸ My <u>luggage</u> is in the boot.

escala *n, f* • eskala   **layover / scale / stopover**

¿Hace alguna <u>escala</u> este vuelo? ▸ Does this flight make any <u>stopver</u>?

estación *n, f* • estaθjOn, estasjOn   **station**

Al llegar a la <u>estación</u>, telefoneé a mi amigo. ▸ On arriving at the <u>station</u>, I called a friend of mine.

estancia *n, f* • estanθja, estansja   **stay**

La conocí durante mi estancia en México. ▸ I met her during my stay in Mexico.

estar de vacaciones *v* • estar de bakasjones **to be on holiday / to be on vacation**

¿Todavía estás de vacaciones? ▸ Are you still on vacation?

excursión *n, f* • ekskursjOn   **excursion / trip**

Marco y Laura se conocieron en una excursión a la montaña. ▸ Marco and Laura met each other on a day trip to the mountain.

extraviar *v* • ekstraβjar   **to lose**

Han extraviado mi maleta. ▸ They lost my suitcase.

facturación *n, f* • fakturaθjOn, fakturasjOn   **check-in**

Vamos al mostrador de facturación. ▸ Let's go to the check-in desk.

facturar *v* • fakturar   **to check in**

Ya he facturado mi equipaje. ▸ I've already checked in my luggage.

ferrocarril *n, m* • ferokaril   **railway**

El ferrocarril siberiano es al mismo tiempo el más largo y el mejor conocido del mundo. ▸ The Siberian Railway is at once the longest and best known railway in the world.

furgoneta *n, f* • furγoneta   **van**

¿Hay espacio para esta caja en la furgoneta? ▸ Is there place for this box in the van?

gasolinera *n, f* • gasolinera   **gas station / petrol station**

Paremos en la próxima gasolinera. ▸ Let's stop at the next gas station.

gastronomía *n, f* • gastronomIa   **gastronomy**

Compré productos únicos en la sección de gastronomía del aeropuerto. ▸ I bought unique food in the gastronomy section of the airport.

globo *n, m* • gloβo   **balloon / globe**

Quiero hacer un viaje en globo. ▸ I want to take a trip in a hot-air-balloon.

guiar *v* • gjaɾ   **to guide / to lead**

¿Quién nos va a guiar? ▸ Who will be guiding us?

helicóptero *n, m* • elikOpteɾo   **helicopter**

El helicóptero está volando muy bajo. ▸ The helicopter is flying very low.

hospedarse *v* • ospeðarse   **to stay**

¿Os vais a hospedar en un hotel? ▸ Are you staying in a hotel?

hostal *n, m* • ostal   **guesthouse / inn**

No pudimos dejar el hostal por el mal tiempo. ▸ We couldn't leave the guest-house because of the bad weather.

huésped *n, f/m* • wEspeð   **guest / lodger**

Los servicios especiales incluyen un chófer personal para cada huésped. ▸

Special services include a personal driver for each guest.

improvisar *v* • improβisar   **to improvise**

¿Planeaste el viaje o simplemente improvisaste? ▸ Did you organize the trip or did you simply improvise?

imprudente *adj* • impruðente   **imprudent / reckless**

Tom es un conductor imprudente. ▸ Tom is a reckless driver.

impuntual *adj* • impuntwal   **late**

¿Por qué siempre eres tan impuntual? ▸ Why are you always late?

impuntualidad *n, f* • impuntwaliðað   **lack of punctuality / lateness**

Vuestra impuntualidad me asombra. ▸ Your lack of punctuality amazes me.

incomodidad *n, f* • iŋkomoðiðað   **discomfort / lack of comfort**

Odio la incomodidad de esperar en los aeropuertos. ▸ I hate the discomfort of waiting at the airport.

incómodo/a *adj* • iŋkOmoðo   **uncomfortable**

Pareces muy incómoda. ▸ You look very uncomfortable.

indemnización *n, f* • indemniθaθjOn, indemnisasjOn   **compensation**

¿Recibiste una compensación tras la cancelación de tu vuelo? ▸ Did you get a compensation after the flight cancellation?

independencia *n, f* • independenθja, independensja   **independence**

Valoro mi independencia, por eso viajo solo. ▸ I value my independence, that's why I travel alone.

independiente *adj* • independjente **independent**

Ella quiere ser más independiente. ▸ She wants to be more independent.

ir de vacaciones *v* • ir de bakasjones **to go on holiday / to go on vacation**

¿Cuándo se va tu hermana de vacaciones? ▸ When is your sister going on holiday?

lejanía *n, f* • lexanIa **distance / remoteness**

Podía divisar una torre en la lejanía. ▸ I made out a tower in the distance.

lejano/a *adj* • lexano **distant / far**

Nuestro destino es todavía muy lejano. ▸ Our destination is still far away.

llegada *n, f* • ʎeɣaða **arrival**

A su llegada a la estación, él llamó un taxi. ▸ On his arrival at the station, he called a taxi.

localizar *v* • lokaliθar, lokalisar **to locate / to spot**

No pudimos localizar a Tom. ▸ We couldn't locate Tom.

maleta *n, f* • maleta **suitcase**

Ayer puse mi maleta en la sala de equipajes, pero ahora parece haberse perdido. ▸ I put my suitcase in the baggage room yesterday, but now it seems to be missing.

marítimo/a *adj* • maɾltima **maritime**

Él conoce muy bien esta ruta marítima. ‣ He knows this maritime route really well.

monumento *n, m* • monumento **monument**

Vamos a visitar los principales monumentos. ‣ We're visiting the main monuments.

motor *n, m* • motoɾ **engine / motor**

Hace una prueba del motor todos los días. ‣ He does an engine test every day.

navegar *v* • naβeɣaɾ **to navigate / to sail**

Me gustaría navegar por todo el mundo. ‣ I'd like to sail around the world.

organizado/a *adj* • oɾɣaniθaðo, oɾɣanisaðo **organized**

El viaje fue organizado por mi jefa. ‣ The trip was organized by my boss.

paisaje *n, m* • paisaxe **landscape / scenery**

Desde el avión, el paisaje no era más que un mosaico de campos. ‣ From the plane, the landscape was just a patchwork of fields.

parada *n, f* • paɾaða **stop**

¿Dónde está la parada de autobús? ‣ Where is the bus stop?

pasajero *n, f/m* • pasaxeɾo **passenger**

Había como mínimo cinco pasajeros a bordo del tren. ▸ There were not less than five passengers on the train.

pasaporte *n, m* • pasaporte **passport**

¿Puedo ver su pasaporte? ▸ May I look at your passport?

pasear *v* • pasear **to take/go for a walk / stroll**

Sacaré a pasear a mi perro. ▸ I'll take my dog out for a walk.

pensión *n, f* • pensjOn **guesthouse**

¿Podría recomendarme una pensión barata? ▸ Could you recommend a cheap guesthouse?

piloto *n, f/m* • piloto **flyer / pilot**

Yo tengo un amigo que es piloto. ▸ I have a friend who is a pilot.

planificar *v* • planifikar **to plan**

Estoy acostumbrado a planificar mi día con anticipación. ▸ I'm used to planning my day in advance.

plano *n, m* • plano **map / plan**

¿Puede usted darme el plano del metro, por favor? ▸ Could I have a subway map, please?

previsión *n, f* • preβisjOn **anticipation / forecast / foresight**

La previsión del tiempo nos anuncia si lloverá o no. ▸ The weather forecast tells us if it will rain or not.

previsor/a *adj* • preβisor **foresighted**

Si fueras previsora, no olvidarías tantas cosas. ▸ If you were foresighted, you wouldn't forget so many things.

primera clase *n, f* • primera klase   **first class**

Estamos más cómodos en primera clase. ▸ We're more comfortable in first class.

pronto *adv* • pronto   **soon**

Volveré pronto. ▸ I will be back soon.

prudente *adj* • pruðente   **careful / prudent**

Nunca se es demasiado prudente cuando se está al volante de un coche. ▸ You cannot be too careful driving a car.

puntual *adj* • puntwal   **punctual**

Me gustaría que fueras más puntual. ▸ I'd like you to be more punctual.

puntualidad *n, f* • puntwaliðað   **punctuality**

Valoramos la puntualidad. ▸ We value punctuality.

recepción *n, f* • reθepθjOn, resepsjOn   **reception / front desk**

La llave se deja en recepción. ▸ Leave the key at the front desk.

reclamación *n, f* • reklamaθjOn, reklamasjOn   **claim / complaint**

Voy a presentar una reclamación por los problemas durante el viaje. ▸ I'm going to present a complaint because of the problems during the trip.

recorrer *v* • rekorer   **to go down / to go through**

Disfrutaba <u>recorriendo</u> caminos en su caballo. ▸ He enjoyed <u>going down</u> paths on his horse.

región *n, f* • rexjOn   **area / region**

Casi nunca llueve en esta <u>región</u>. ▸ It hardly ever rains in the <u>area</u>.

reserva *n, f* • reserβa   **booking / reservation / reserve**

Me gustaría cambiar mi <u>reserva</u>. ▸ I'd like to change my <u>reservation</u>.

reservar *v* • reserβar   **to book / to reserve**

Quisiera <u>reservar</u> un asiento en este tren. ▸ I'd like to <u>reserve</u> a seat on this train.

reunión *n, f* • reunjOn   **meeting / reunion**

Se ha cancelado la <u>reunión</u> de hoy. ▸ Today's <u>meeting</u> has been canceled.

ruido *n, m* • rwiðo   **noise**

Estoy acostumbrado al <u>ruido</u>. ▸ I'm used to the <u>noise</u>.

rural *adj* • rural   **rural**

¿Alguna vez has vivido en un sector <u>rural</u>? ▸ Have you ever lived in a <u>rural</u> area?

ruta *n, f* • ruta   **route**

Quisiera un mapa con las <u>rutas</u> de los buses. ▸ I'd like a bus <u>route</u> map.

saco de dormir *n, m* • sako de dormir   **sleeping bag**

Necesitamos <u>sacos de dormir</u> para acampar. ▸ We need <u>sleeping bags</u> in order to camp.

salida *n, f* • saliða   **departure / exit**

Tienes que posponer tu salida a Inglaterra hasta la próxima semana. ▸ You
have to put off your departure for England till next week.

silencio *n, m* • silenθjo, silensjo   **hush / quiet / silence**

Todo es silencio alrededor. ▸ All around is silence.

situado/a *adj* • sitwaðo   **located**

Este hotel está muy bien situado en lo que concierne al transporte público.
▸ This hotel is conveniently located in terms of public transportation.

souvenir *n, m* • souβenir   **souvenir**

Este será un buen souvenir de mi viaje a los Estados Unidos. ▸ This will be
a good souvenir of my trip around the United States.

tardar *v* • tarðar   **to be late / take time**

Tal vez quieras sentarte. Esto va a tardar un rato. ▸ You might want to sit
down. This is going to take a while.

tarde *adv / n, f* • tarðe   **afternoon / evening / late**

Perdona que llegue tarde. ▸ I'm sorry I'm late.

terrestre *adj* • terestre   **overland / terrestrial**

Hay que hacer cambios importantes en el transporte terrestre del país. ▸ Important changes must be made when it comes to overland transport in the

country.

tienda de campaña *n, f* • tjenda de kampaɲa   **tent**

Necesitamos una tienda de campaña más grande. ▸ We need a bigger tent.

tráfico *n, m* • tɾАfiko   **traffic**

Hay mucho tráfico en este camino. ▸ There is heavy traffic on this road.

transportar *v* • transportaɾ   **to carry / to transport**

Este avión es capaz de transportar a 40 personas cada vez. ▸ This airplane
is capable of carrying 40 passengers at a time.

tranvía *n, m* • tɾambІa   **tram / streetcar**

¿Qué es más barato, el autobús o el tranvía? ▸ Which is cheaper, the bus or
the streetcar?

trasladar *v* • tɾazlaðaɾ   **to move / to transfer**

¿Por qué te trasladaste a otra casa? ▸ Why did you move to another house?

traslado *n, m* • tɾazlaðo   **move / relocation / transfer**

La caja se rompió durante el traslado a la nueva casa. ▸ The box broke during the move to the new house.

trayecto *n, m* • tɾajekto   **journey / route**

Me sentí enferma todo el trayecto. ▸ I felt sick the whole journey.

vehículo *n, m* • beІkulo   **vehicle**

Es difícil decir cuál vehículo es más bello. ▸ It is difficult to say which vehicle is more beautiful.

velocidad *n, f* • beloθiðað, belosiðað   **speed**

No excedas la máxima velocidad. ▸ Don't exceed the speed limit.

viaje de negocios *n, m* • bjaxe de neɣosjos   **business trip**

Mi madre está en un viaje de negocios. ▸ My mother is on a business trip.

viajero/a *n, m/f* • bjaxero   **traveler**

Un viajero me paró para preguntarme el camino. ▸ The traveler stopped to ask me the way.

vuelo *n, m* • bwelo   **flight**

¿Hay un vuelo por la tarde? ▸ Is there a flight in the afternoon?

vuelo chárter *n, m* • bwelo ʧArter   **charter flight**

Tomamos un vuelo chárter a Madrid. ▸ We took a charter flight to Madrid.

11 Career & Workplace

actualizar v • aktwaliθaɾ, aktwalisaɾ   **to update**

¿Me podrías <u>actualizar</u> estos datos? ▸ Could I get you to <u>update</u> this data for me?

acuerdo n, m • akweɾðo   **agreement / deal**

Los detalles del <u>acuerdo</u> quedan establecidos en el contrato. ▸ The details of the <u>agreement</u> are set forth in the contract.

adecuado/a adj • aðekwaðo   **adequate / appropriate / proper**

Si no logramos un conocimiento <u>adecuado</u> de su cultura, podrían surgir muchos problemas con facilidad. ▸ If we don't obtain an <u>adequate</u> knowledge of their culture, a lot of problems could easily arise.

administración n, f • aðministɾaθjOn, aðministɾasjOn   **administration / management / running**

Su hijo asumió la <u>administración</u> de la fábrica. ▸ His son took on the <u>management</u> of the factory.

administrar v • aðministɾaɾ   **to administer / to manage / to run**

Quisiera <u>administrar</u> una gran explotación ganadera. ▸ I'd like to <u>run</u> a big stock farm.

administrativo/a *adj* • aðministratiβo   **administrative**

Juan es el gerente administrativo del banco. ▸ Juan is the bank's administrative manager.

agruparse *v* • aɣruparse   **to form a group**

Vamos a agruparnos adecuadamente. ▸ Let's form a group properly.

ambición *n, f* • ambiθjOn, ambisjOn   **ambition / thirst**

Su ambición es ser abogado. ▸ His ambition is to be a lawyer.

ambicioso/a *adj* • ambiθjoso, ambisjoso   **ambitious**

Es un proyecto ambicioso. ▸ It's an ambitious project.

anuncio de trabajo *n, m* • anunsjo de traβaxo   **job advertisement**

Este anuncio de trabajo ha recibido numerosas respuestas. ▸ This job advertisement has received several responses.

artesanal *adj* • artesanal   **craft / handmade**

Vendo mi propia cerveza artesanal. ▸ I sell my own craft beer.

asalariado/a *adj* • asalarjaðo   **salaried**

Soy un simple empleado asalariado. ▸ I'm just a salaried employee.

baja por enfermedad *n, f* • baxa por emfermeðað   **sick leave**

Ella ha estado de baja por enfermedad dos meses. ▸ She has been on sick leave for two months.

baja por maternidad *n, f* • baxa por materniðað   **maternity leave**

¿Aún estás de baja por maternidad? ▸ Are you still on maternity leave?

baja por paternidad *n, f* • baxa por paterniðað   **paternity leave**

¿Cuánto tiempo estarás de baja por paternidad? ▸ How long are you going to be on paternity leave?

bienestar *n, m* • bjenestar   **welfare / well-being**

Él trabaja por el bienestar social. ▸ He is working for social welfare.

buscar trabajo *v* • buskar traβaxo   **to look for a job / to seek employment**

Llevo un mes buscando trabajo. ▸ I've been seeking employment for a month.

candidato/a *n, f/m* • kandiðato   **candidate**

Todavía no han contratado a ningún candidato. ▸ They haven't hired any candidate yet.

cargo *n, m* • karɣo   **charge / post / position**

Él está a cargo del departamento de ventas. ▸ He's in charge of the sales department.

carrera *n, f* • karera   **career / race**

Poco después de volver a Francia decidió abandonar su carrera de economista para dedicarse a su verdadera pasión, la escritura, en España. ▸ Shortly after coming back to France, he decided to abandon his career as an economist in order to dedicate himself to his true passion: writing, in Spain.

carta de recomendación *n, f* • kaṛta de rekomendasjOn   **recommendation letter**

Tener una carta de recomendación puede ser útil. ▸ Having a recommendation letter might be useful.

cobrar *v* • koβɾaɾ   **to charge / to get paid**

¿Cuándo voy a cobrar? ▸ When do I get paid?

compañero/a *n, f/m* • kompaɲeɾo   **colleague / partner**

"¿Quién vendrá a la fiesta?" "Unos pocos amigos y cuatro o cinco compañeros de trabajo." ▸ "Who will be coming to the party?" "A few friends and four or five colleagues."

compensación *n, f* • kompensaθjOn, kompensasjOn   **compensation**

Te prometo toda posible compensación. ▸ I promise you every possible compensation.

complicación *n, f* • komplikaθjOn, komplikasjOn   **complication / hassle**

El plan presenta algunas complicaciones. ▸ THe plan has some complications.

complicado/a *adj* • komplikaðo   **complicated**

El mecanismo de esta máquina es complicado. ▸ The mechanism of this machine is complicated.

concentración *n, f* • konθentraθjOn, konsentrasjOn   **concentration**

Éste es el tipo de trabajo que requiere un alto nivel de concentración. ▸ This is the kind of work that requires a high level of <u>concentration</u>.

concentrado/a *adj* • konθentraðo, konsentraðo   **concentrated / focused**

Soy incapaz de permanecer <u>concentrado</u>. ▸ I'm incapable of staying <u>focused</u>.

concentrarse *v* • konθentrarse, konsentrarse   **to concentrate / to focus**

Todo lo que hay que hacer es <u>concentrarse</u>. ▸ All you have to do is to <u>con-</u><u>centrate</u>.

condición *n, f* • kondiθjOn, kondisjOn   **condition**

Sólo aceptaremos bajo esa <u>condición</u>. ▸ We will only consent on that <u>condi-</u><u>tion</u>.

conforme *adj* • komforme   **in agreement / satisfied**

¿Estás <u>conforme</u> con nuestras condiciones? ▸ Are you <u>satisfied</u> con our con-ditions?

contratación *n, f* • kontrataθjOn, kontratasjOn   **contracting / hiring / recruitment**

Estamos en periodo de <u>contratación</u>. ▸ It's <u>hiring</u> period.

contratar *v* • kontratar   **to contract / to employ / to hire**

No puedo <u>contratar</u> un conductor. No tengo dinero para ello. ▸ I cannot <u>hire</u> a driver. I don't have money for that.

contrato *n, m* • kontrato   **agreement / contract**

En vez de esperar un <u>contrato</u>, podemos tratarlo por teléfono. ▸ Instead of waiting for a <u>contract</u>, we can handle it over the phone.

control *n, m* • kontrol   **control**

Lo tengo todo bajo <u>control</u>. ▸ I have everything under <u>control</u>.

coordinación *n, f* • koorðinaθjOn, koorðinasjOn   **coordination**

Vuestra <u>coordinación</u> es admirable. ▸ Your <u>coordination</u> is remarkable.

coordinador/a *n, f/m* • koorðinaðor   **coordinator**

¿Puedo hablar con el <u>coordinador</u> del evento? ▸ May I speak with the event <u>coordinator</u>?

coordinar *v* • koorðinar   **to coordinate**

¿Quién va a <u>coordinar</u> nuestra actividad, si nosotros mismos no lo hacemos? ▸ Who is going to <u>coordinate</u> our activity if we don't do it for ourselves?

corporación *n, f* • korporaθjOn, korporasjOn   **corporation**

Desacuerdos departamentales llevaron a que la <u>corporación</u> se dividiera en cinco compañías separadas. ▸ Departmental disagreements led the <u>corporation</u> to split into five separate companies.

curriculum vitae *n, m* • kurikulum bitae   **CV / resumé**

Me gustaría enviarles mi <u>currículum vitae</u>. ▸ I'd like to send you my <u>CV</u>.

datos personales *n, m* • datos personales   **personal details**

¿Podría rellenar esta sección con sus <u>datos personales</u>? ▸ Could you fill in this section with your <u>personal details</u>?

departamento *n, m* • departamento   **department**

Ella se convirtió en la directora del departamento de cardiología del hospital de la ciudad. ‣ She became the director of the cardiology department at the city hospital.

descanso *n, m* • deskanso   **break / rest**

Reanudó su trabajo tras un breve descanso. ‣ He resumed his work after a short break.

desconectar *v* • deskonektar   **to switch off**

Creo que tienes que desconectar del trabajo y divertirte. ‣ I think you have to switch off from work and have some fun.

descontrol *n, m* • deskontrol   **chaos / turmoil**

Nuestro jefe no aceptará este descontrol. ‣ Our boss won't accept this chaos.

desempleo *n, m* • desempleo   **unemployment**

Este año el desempleo alcanzará niveles récord. ‣ This year unemployment will reach record levels.

despedir *v* • despeðir   **to dismiss / to fire**

Tuvieron que despedir a 300 hombres de la fábrica. ‣ They had to fire 300 men at the factory.

despido *n, m* • despiðo   **dismissal / firing / redundancy**

¿Cuál es la causa de tu despido? ‣ What's the cause of your dismissal?

dificultar *v* • difikultar   **to complicate / to make difficult**

Su comportamiento dificultó el proceso de despido. ‣ Her behavior complicated the dismissal process.

director/a *n, f/m* • direktor   **director**

¿De qué color y de qué marca es el coche del director? ▸ What brand and what color is the director's car?

dirigir *v* • dirixir   **to direct / to manage / to run**

Algunos miembros de la junta cuestionaron su habilidad para dirigir la corporación. ▸ Some board members questioned his ability to run the corporation.

disponibilidad *n, f* • disponiβiliðað   **availability**

Contáctenos para confirmar la disponibilidad. ▸ Contact us to check availability.

disponible *adj* • disponiβle   **available / free**

El doctor sólo está disponible los días laborables. ▸ The doctor is only available on weekdays.

echar *v* • etʃar   **to sack**

¿Es verdad que te han echado? ▸ Is it true that you've been sacked?

empleado/a *n, f/m* • empleaðo   **employee**

El jefe está pensando en despedir a un empleado. ▸ The boss is thinking of firing an employee.

empleo *n, m* • empleo   **employment / job**

¿Qué clase de empleo busca usted? ▸ What type of job are you looking for?

empresa *n, f* • empɾesa   **business / company / entrerprise**

Él ha fundado una empresa recientemente. ▸ He set up a company recently.

empresario/a *n, f/m* • empɾesaɾjo   **business owner**

Mi hija quiere ser empresaria. ▸ My daughter wants to be a business owner.

equipo *n, m* • ekipo   **team**

No me gusta trabajar en equipo. ▸ I don't like playing on a team.

experiencia *n, f* • ekspeɾjenθja, ekspeɾjensja   **experience**

¿Tiene experiencia profesional? ▸ Do you have professional experience?

facilitar *v* • faθilitaɾ, fasilitaɾ   **to facilitate / to make easier**

Hemos establecido el instituto con el fin de facilitar la investigación. ▸ We have established the institute with a view to facilitating the research.

financiar *v* • finanθjaɾ, finansjaɾ   **to finance / to fund**

¿Quién va a financiar vuestro proyecto? ▸ Who is going to fund your project?

firmar *v* • fiɾmaɾ   **to sign**

¿Alguna vez has firmado un contrato? ▸ Have you ever signed a contract?

flexible *adj* • fleksiβle   **flexible**

Tengo un horario flexible. ▸ I have a flexible schedule.

formación *n, f* • formaθjOn, formasjOn   **training**

Les ofrecemos la oportunidad de obtener una formación en ciencias matemáticas. ▸ We offer you the chance to obtain training in the mathematical sciences.

fundador/a *adj* • fundaðoɾ   **founder / founding**

La universidad lleva el nombre de su fundador. ▸ The university bears the name of its founder.

fundamental *adj* • fundamental   **fundamental**

Esta es una pregunta fundamental. ▸ This is a fundamental question.

fundar *v* • fundaɾ   **to found**

¿Cuándo se fundó esta empresa? ▸ When was this company founded?

ganarse la vida *v* • ganaɾse la biða   **to make a living**

¿Cómo te ganas la vida en España? ▸ How do you make a living in Spain?

gerente *n, f/m* • xeɾente   **manager**

Quiero ver al gerente. ▸ I want to see the manager.

grado *n, m* • gɾaðo   **degree / grade**

Con un grado universitario, Tom conseguirá un mejor empleo. ▸ Tom will get a better job with a college degree.

graduado/a *n, f/m* • gɾaðwaðo   **graduate**

Se ha graduado en Harvard. ▸ She graduated from Harvard.

hacer prácticas v • aser prAktikas   **to do an internship**

¿Dónde estás haciendo las prácticas? ▸ Where are you doing your intern-ship?

horas extraordinarias n, f • oras ekstraorðinarjas   **overtime**

Me temo que tendré que hacer horas extraordinarias para poder ahorrar algo de dinero. ▸ I'm afraid I have to do overtime to be able to save some money.

horas extras n, f • oras ekstras   **overtime**

Ella está haciendo horas extras porque necesita el dinero. ▸ She is doing some overtime because she needs the money.

huelga n, f • welga   **strike**

Los trabajadores están en huelga. ▸ The workers are on strike.

inadecuado/a adj • inaðekwaðo   **inadequate / inappropriate**

Su vocabulario es inadecuado. ▸ His vocabulary is inadequate.

incapacidad n, f • iŋkapaθiðað, iŋkapasiðað   **disability / inability / incapacity**

Su incapacidad para tomar decisiones me impacienta. ▸ I am impatient with his inability to make decisions.

incorporación n, f • iŋkorporaθjOn, iŋkorporasjOn   **incorporation**

Necesitamos algunos documentos antes de su incorporación. ▸ We need some documents before her incorporation.

indefinido/a *adj* • indefiniðo   **indefinite**

Ella tiene un contrato indefinido. ▸ She has an indefinite contract.

indemnizar *v* • indemniθar, indemnisar   **to compensate**

La compañía de seguros me indemnizó después del accidente. ▸ The insurance company compensated me after the accident.

individual *adj* • indiβiðwal   **individual**

Estamos especializados en el asesoramiento individual de nuestros clientes. ▸ We are specialized in the individual consultation of our customers.

interrupción *n, f* • interupθjOn, interupsjOn   **interruption**

Lamento la interrupción. ▸ Sorry for the interruption.

irregular *adj* • ireɣular   **irregular**

Su asistencia es irregular. ▸ His attendance is irregular.

jefe/a *n, f/m* • xefe   **boss / chief**

Mi jefe rechazó el presupuesto para el nuevo proyecto. ▸ My boss rejected the budget for the new project.

jerarquía *n, f* • xerarkIa   **hierarchy**

Siempre hemos tenido una firme jerarquía en este equipo. ▸ We've always had a strict hierarchy in this team.

jornada *n, f* • xornaða   **day**

Un buen café con leche por la mañana te despabila para toda la jornada. ▸
A good coffee with milk in the morning will wake you up for the day.

jornada completa *n, f* • xoɾnaða kompleta   **full-time**

María tiene un trabajo de jornada completa. ▸ María has a full-time job.

jornada partida *n, f* • xoɾnaða paɾtiða   **split shift**

Esta semana tenemos jornada partida en el trabajo. ▸ We have a split shift
at work this week.

jubilación *n, f* • xuβilaθjOn, xuβilasjOn   **retirement**

Por supuesto, muchos ciudadanos de la tercera edad son felices con la jubilación. ▸ Of course, many senior citizens are happy with retirement.

jubilado/a *adj* • xuβilaðo   **retired**

Mis padres están jubilados y por eso viajan tanto. ▸ My parents are retired,
that's why they travel so often.

licenciado/a *adj* • liθenθjaðo, lisensjaðo   **graduate**

Somos licenciados en derecho. ▸ We are law school graduates.

licenciatura *n, f* • liθenθjatuɾa, lisensjatuɾa   **degree**

Mi hermana tiene una licenciatura en biología. ▸ My sister has a degree in
biology.

mejorar *v* • mexoɾaɾ   **to improve**

La compañía está tratando de mejorar su imagen. ▸ The company is trying to improve its image.

movilidad *n, f* • moβiliðað   **mobility**

Al equipo le faltó movilidad. ▸ The team lacked mobility.

nómina *n, f* • nOmina   **payroll**

El gerente quiere comprobar la nómina de todos los empleados. ▸ The manager wants to check every employee's payroll.

nuevas tecnologías *n, f* • nweβas teknoloxIas   **new technologies**

La adopción de nuevas tecnologías es fundamental para nosotros. ▸ The adoption of new technologies is key for us.

obligación *n, f* • oβliɣaθjOn, oβliɣasjOn   **duty / obligation**

Es tu obligación terminar el trabajo. ▸ It's your duty to finish the job.

obligar *v* • oβliɣaɾ   **to force / to oblige**

No me puedes obligar a hacer algo que no quiero. ▸ You can't force me to do anything I don't want to do.

obligatorio/a *adj* • oβliɣatorjo   **compulsory / mandatory**

Lo siento, es obligatorio terminar antes de las 5. ▸ I'm sorry, it's mandatory to finish before 5.

oficial *adj* • ofiθjal, ofisjal   **official**

Esta noticia es oficial. ▸ This news is official.

oficina de empleo *n, f* • ofisina de empleo   **job center**

Cuando estaba en paro, iba a la oficina de empleo cada semana. ▸ When I was unemployed, I used to go to the job center every week.

oficio *n, m* • ofiθjo, ofisjo   **profession / trade**

Yo conozco mi oficio. ▸ I know my trade.

paciencia *n, f* • paθjenθja, pasjensja   **patience**

Tenga paciencia por uno o dos días más. ▸ Have patience for another day or two.

paga *n, f* • paɣa   **allowance / pay / pocket money**

Su padre puede permitirse el darle una gran paga cada mes. ▸ Her father can afford to give her a big allowance every month.

parado/a *adj* • paraðo   **unemployed**

Actualmente, Tom está parado. ▸ Tom is currently unemployed.

paro *n, m* • paɾo   **unemployment**

Ha subido el paro. ▸ Unemployment has risen.

pensión *n, f* • pensjOn   **pension**

Las personas de 65 años o más reciben una pensión del Gobierno. ▸ People of 65 and above get a pension from the government.

pensionista *adj* • pensjonista   **pensioner / retiree**

Como soy pensionista, por fin soy mi propio jefe. ▸ As a pensioner, I'm my own boss now, finally.

perder el trabajo *v* • perðer el traβaxo   **to lose your job**

Siento que hayas perdido tu trabajo. ▸ I'm sorry you lost your job.

personal *n, m* • personal   **staff**

Debido a la escasez de trabajo, la mitad del personal fue dada de baja. ▸ Because of a shortage of work, half the staff was discharged.

plantilla *n, f* • plantiʎa   **staff / workforce**

Quisiera agradecer a la plantilla de ambas organizaciones por el trabajo realizado. ▸ I'd like to thank the staff of both organizations for all the work done.

profesional *adj* • profesjonal   **professional**

Mary es una bailarina profesional. ▸ Mary is a professional dancer.

progresar *v* • proɣresar   **to make progress / to progress**

Nuestros proyectos no están progresando como deberían. ▸ Our projects are not progressing as they should.

propósito *n, m* • propOsito   **goal / purpose / target**

¿Cuál es el propósito de su visita? ▸ What's the purpose of your visit?

protestar *v* • protestar   **to complain / to protest**

Los trabajadores han decidido protestar. ▸ The workers decided to protest.

proyecto *n, m* • projekto   **project / scheme**

Estoy orgulloso de formar parte de este proyecto. ▸ I am proud to be a part of this project.

puntualidad *n, f* • puntwaliðað   **punctuality**

Él está orgulloso de su puntualidad. ▸ He is proud of his punctuality.

recursos humanos *n, m* • rekursos umanos   **human resources**

¿Quién se encarga de recursos humanos en la oficina? ▸ Who is in charge of human resources at the office?

regular *v* • reɣular   **to regulate**

Las actividades comerciales están reguladas por la ley. ▸ Business activities are regulated by the law.

requisito *n, m* • rekisito   **requirement**

Este trabajo no cumple con nuestros requisitos. ▸ This work does not meet our requirements.

reunirse *v* • reunirse   **to gather / to join / to meet**

Está ocupado y no puede reunirse contigo. ▸ He's busy and can't meet with you.

revolución *n, f* • reβoluθjOn, reβolusjOn   **revolution**

La revolución introdujo una nueva era. ▸ The revolution ushered in a new era.

revolucionario/a *adj* • reβoluθjonarjo, reβolusjonarjo   **revolutionary**

El consejo revolucionario se reunió para planear la estrategia. ▸ The revolutionary council met to plan the strategy.

salario *n, m* • salarjo   **salary / wage**

Él siempre está quejándose de su bajo salario. ▸ He is always complaining about his low salary.

socio/a *n, f/m* • soθjo, sosjo   **partner**

Quiero que seas mi socio. ▸ I want you to be my partner.

sueldo *n, m* • sweldo   **salary / wage**

El sueldo va en función de la edad y la experiencia. ▸ The salary is fixed according to age and experience.

sustituir *v* • sustitwir   **to substitute / replace**

No pudimos encontrar a nadie para sustituir a Oliver. ▸ We couldn't find anyone to replace Oliver.

temporal *adj* • temporal   **temporary**

Le aseguro que esto solo es temporal. ▸ I assure you this is only temporary.

tiempo parcial *n, m* • tjempo parsjal   **part-time**

Tengo hijos, por eso trabajo a tiempo parcial. ▸ I have children, that's why I work part-time.

trabajador/a *n, f/m* • traβaxaðor   **worker**

Pidieron que el joven trabajador dimitiese. ▸ The young worker was asked to resign.

trabajador/a autónomo/a *n, f/m* • traβaxaðor autOnomo   **freelancer**

Estoy harta de trabajar en esta empresa. Prefiero ser una trabajadora autónoma.
▸ I'm tired of working in this company. I prefer to be a freelancer.

trabajo fijo *n, m* • traβaxo fixo   **steady job**

Mi hijo consiguió por fin un trabajo fijo. ▸ My son got a steady job at last.

trabajo temporal *n, m* • traβaxo temporal   **temporary employment**

La empresa de trabajo temporal me ayudó a conseguir mi primer empleo. ▸
The temporary employment agency helped me get my first job.

vago/a *adj* • baγo   **lazy**

Él no es vago, al contrario, pienso que trabaja duro. ▸ He's not lazy. On the
contrary, I think he's a hard worker.

valorar *v* • balorar   **to value**

Ella valora más la salud que la riqueza. ▸ She values health above wealth.

viaje de negocios *n, m* • bjaxe de neγosjos   **business trip**

Carla está en un viaje de negocios hasta el viernes. ▸ Carla is on a business
trip until Friday.

zona *n, f* • θona, sona   **area / zone**

En esta zona está prohibido fumar. ▸ Smoking is forbidden in this area.

12 Nature & Environment

ahorrar v • aorar   **to economize / to save**

Debemos ahorrar electricidad. ▸ We must save electricity.

alimentar v • alimentar   **to feed**

¿Tienes algo de pan? Voy a alimentar a las palomas. ▸ Do you have some bread? I'm going to feed the pigeons.

alimento n, m • alimento   **food**

La carne roja es un alimento proteico. ▸ Red meat is a high-protein food.

arar v • arar   **to plough / to plow**

Voy a arar esta tierra con el tractor nuevo. ▸ I'm going to plow this piece of land with the new tractor.

aumentar v • aumentar   **to increase / to rise**

La población mundial tiende a aumentar. ▸ The world's population tends to increase.

aumento n, m • aumento   **increase / rise**

Este extraordinario aumento se explica por la veloz unificación económica que tuvo lugar durante el mismo período. ▸ This extraordinary increase is explained by the speedy economic unification which took place during the same period.

ave *n, f* • aβe   **bird**

El niño liberó al ave de la jaula. ▸ The boy released a bird from the cage.

basura *n, f* • basura   **garbage / junk / litter / rubbish / trash**

¿Cuántas veces a la semana se recoge la basura en esta ciudad? ▸ How many times a week do they collect garbage in this town?

beneficiar *v* • benefiθjar, benefisjar   **to benefit**

Todos nos podemos beneficiar de su experiencia. ▸ We can all benfit from his experience.

beneficio *n, m* • benefiθjo, benefisjo   **benefit / profit**

Será por nuestro mutuo beneficio seguir el plan. ▸ It will be to our mutual benefit to carry out the plan.

beneficioso/a *adj* • benefiθjoso, benefisjoso   **beneficial**

Beber suficiente agua es beneficioso para la salud. ▸ Drinking plenty of water is beneficial to your health.

calentamiento global *n, m* • kalentamjento gloβal   **global warming**

El calentamiento global es una triste realidad. ▸ Global warming is a sad reality.

campesino *n, f/m* • kampesino   **farmer / peasant**

Esos campesinos necesitan urgentemente tierra para cultivar arroz. ▸ Those peasants badly need land to grow rice.

cartón *n, m* • kartOn   **cardboard / carton**

Esta caja está hecha de cartón. ▸ This box is made of cardboard.

catástrofe *n, f* • katAstrofe   **catastrophe**

Debemos evitar una catástrofe similar a esta. ▸ We have to avoid another catastrophe similar to this one.

césped *n, m* • θEspeð, sEspeð   **grass**

El jardinero no deja que pisemos el césped. ▸ The gardener didn't let us walk on the grass.

climático/a *adj* • klimAtiko   **climate / climatic**

Los hielos del sur de Argentina están sufriendo los efectos del cambio climático. ▸ The ice of southern Argentina is suffering from the effects of climate change.

combustible *n, m* • kombustiβle   **fuel**

Contaminantes como éste derivan principalmente de la quema de combustibles en motores de vehículos. ▸ Pollutants like this derive mainly from the combustion of fuel in car engines.

concienciado *adj* • konθjenθjaðo, konsjensjaðo   **aware**

Estamos muy concienciados del problema medioambiental de nuestra región. ▸ We are fully aware of the environmental problem in our region.

conservación *n, f* • konserβaθjOn, konserβasjOn   **conservation**

Sólo recientemente la gente se ha empezado a dar cuenta de la importancia de la conservación de la naturaleza. ▸ It is only recently that people have begun to realize the importance of nature conservation.

conservar *v* • konserβar   **to conserve / to preserve**

Conservar las tradiciones es normal en casi todas las culturas. ▸ Preserving traditions is normal in almost all cultures.

consumir *v* • konsumir   **to consume / to use**

Quiero que mi vida sea más, a fin de cuentas, que simplemente consumir productos y generar basura. ▸ I want my life to amount to more than just consuming products and generating garbage.

consumismo *n, m* • konsumizmo   **consumerism**

El consumismo exacerbado en algunos países afecta al entorno natural. ▸ Excessive consumerism in some countries affects the natural environment.

contaminación *n, f* • kontaminaθjOn, kontaminasjOn **contamination / pollution**

La contaminación está dañando nuestra tierra. ▸ Pollution is damaging our earth.

contenedor *n, m* • konteneðor   **bin / container**

Usa el contenedor para la basura. ▸ Use the trash bin.

cortar *v* • kortar   **to cut**

Necesito unas tijeras para cortar este papel. ▸ I need a pair of scissors to cut this paper.

cosecha *n, f* • kosetʃa   **harvest**

La buena cosecha bajó el precio del arroz. ▸ The good harvest brought down the price of rice.

costa *n, f* • kosta   **coast / seaside**

El barco navegó por la costa. ▸ The ship sailed along the coast.

cultivar *v* • kultiβaɾ   **to cultivate / to grow**

Voy a cultivar trigo allí. ▸ I'm going to grow wheat there.

cumbre *n, f* • kumbɾe   **summit / top**

Vista desde la cumbre de la colina, la isla es muy bonita. ▸ Seen from the top of the hill, the island is very beautiful.

dañar *v* • daɲaɾ   **to damage / to harm**

La falta de ejercicio puede dañar tu salud. ▸ Lack of exercise may harm your health.

dañino/a *adj* • daɲino   **damaging / harmful**

Fumar es dañino para la salud. ▸ Smoking is harmful to health.

daño *n, m* • daɲo   **damage / harm**

Dondequiera que mires podrás observar el daño causado por el terremoto. ▸ Everywhere you look you can see damage caused by the earthquake.

desaparición *n, f* • desapaɾiθjOn, desapaɾisjOn   **disappearance**

Los científicos están debatiendo su teoría acerca de la desaparición de los dinosaurios. ▸ Scientists are debating his theory about the disappearance of the dinosaurs.

descuidado/a *adj* • deskwiðaðo   **careless / neglected**

Me arrepiento de haber descuidado mi salud. ▸ I regret having neglected my health.

deshielo *n, m* • desjelo   **melting / thaw**

Ya vemos los efectos negativos del deshielo. ▸ We already see the negative effects of melting.

desierto *n, m* • desjerto   **desert**

Los camellos se usan a menudo para viajar por el desierto. ▸ Camels are often used to travel in the desert.

despejado/a *adj* • despexaðo   **clear**

El cielo está despejado casi todos los días. ▸ The sky is clear almost every day.

desprotegido/a *adj* • desprotexiðo   **unprotected**

Actualmente hay cientos de millas de costa desprotegida en nuestro país. ▸ Nowadays there are thousands of miles of unprotected coast in our country.

disponible *adj* • disponiβle   **available**

Tenemos poco dinero disponible para la investigación. ▸ We have little money available for the research.

ecología *n, f* • ekoloxIa   **ecology**

Le hice muchas preguntas sobre la ecología. ▸ I asked him many questions about ecology.

ecológico/a *adj* • ekolOxiko   **ecological / environmentally friendly**

La bioclimática es un acercamiento ecológico a la arquitectura. ▸ Bioclimatic is an ecological approach to architecture.

ecosistema *n, m* • ekosistema   **ecosystem / environment**

La construcción de la presa creó un lago artificial que destruyó todo un ecosistema. ▸ The construction of the dam created an artificial lake that destroyed a whole ecosystem.

eficaz *adj* • efikaθ, efikas   **effective / efficient**

Mi método es sorprendentemente simple, pero muy eficaz. ▸ My method is surprisingly simple, but highly effective.

eficiente *adj* • efiθjente, efisjente   **efficient**

Nuestro motor es más eficiente y produce mucho menos CO2. ▸ Our engine is efficient and produces much less CO2.

empeorar *v* • empeorar   **to aggravate / worsen**

La situación de estos animales está empeorando. ▸ The condition of these animals is worsening.

energía eléctrica *n, f* • enerxIa elEktrika   **electrical energy**

Esto transforma la energía eléctrica en lumínica. ▸ This transforms electrical energy into light.

energía eólica *n, f* • enerxIa eOlika   **wind energy**

¿Cómo se genera la energía eólica? ▸ How is wind energy generated?

energía solar *n, f* • enerxIa solar   **solar energy**

La energía solar es cada vez más popular. ▸ Solar energy is more and more popular.

envasar *v* • embasar   **to pack**

¿Habéis envasado la fruta? ▸ Have you packed the fruit?

equilibrio *n, m* • ekiliβrjo   **balance / equilibrium**

Es un equilibrio muy delicado. ▸ It's a very delicate balance.

fabricación *n, f* • faβrikaθjOn, faβrikasjOn   **fabrication / manufacturing**

La fabricación de nuestros productos es muy compleja. ▸ Manufacturing our products is very complex.

fabricar *v* • faβrikar   **to make up / to manufacture**

¿Qué productos fabrican aquí? ▸ What kind of products do they manufacture here?

falta *n, f* • falta   **absence / lack / shortage**

Esta falta de responsabilidad me está volviendo loco. ▸ This lack of responsibility is driving me crazy.

gas *n, m* • gas   **gas**

La explosión pudo haber sido causada por una fuga de gas. ▸ The explosion may have been caused by a gas leak.

gastar *v* • gastar   **to spend**

De aquí en adelante tendremos que gastar menos. ▸ From now on, we'll have to spend less money.

gasto *n, m* • gasto   **expense / expenditure / maintenance**

Algunos gastos son imposibles de evitar. ▸ Some expenses are impossible to avoid.

geografía *n, f* • xeoɣrafĩa   **geography**

Le gusta la geografía y la historia. ▸ He likes geography and history.

granja *n, f* • graŋxa   **farm**

Era lo suficientemente fuerte como para ayudar a su padre en la granja. ▸ He was strong enough to help his father on the farm.

hoja *n, f* • oxa   **leaf / sheet**

Una hoja seca se cayó al suelo. ▸ A dead leaf fell to the ground.

horizonte *n, m* • oriθonte, orisonte   **horizon**

El mar se fundía con el cielo en el horizonte. ▸ The ocean melted into the sky on the horizon.

huerto *n, m* • werto   **orchard / vegetable garden**

El huerto parecía desaliñado después de ser golpeado por una temprana helada. ▸ The vegetable garden looked bedraggled after being hit by an early frost.

impulsar *v* • impulsar   **to boost / to urge**

¿Cómo podríamos impulsar la economía? ▸ How could we boost the economy?

iniciativa *n, f* • iniθjatiβa, inisjatiβa   **enterprise / initiative**

El presidente instó a los empleados a unirse a su iniciativa. ▸ The president
urged the employees to act on their initiative.

inmoral *adj* • immoral   **immoral**

Algunas personas piensan que comer carne es inmoral. ▸ Some people think
that eating meat is immoral.

innecesario/a *adj* • inneθesarjo, innesesarjo   **pointless / unnecessary**

Si piensas que reciclar es innecesario, te equivocas. ▸ If you think that recycling is unnecessary, you're wrong.

insecto *n, m* • insekto   **insect**

El pájaro intenta capturar al insecto. ▸ The bird is trying to get the insect.

invisible *adj* • imbisiβle   **invisible**

La materia oscura es invisible. ▸ Dark matter is invisible.

jaula *n, f* • xaula   **birdcage / cage**

El león luchó para salir de su jaula. ▸ The lion struggled to get out of his
cage.

ladera *n, f* • laðera   **mountainside**

Me encantaría tener una cabaña en esta ladera. ▸ I'd love to have a cottage
on this mountainside.

lata *n, f* • lata   **can / tin**

Esta caja está hecha de lata. ▸ This box is made of tin.

legumbres *n, f* • leɣumbres   **pulses**

Como legumbres dos veces por semana. ▸ I eat pulses twice per week.

libre *adj* • liβre   **free**

Nos oponemos al comercio libre. ▸ We stand against free trade.

limpieza *n, f* • limpjeθa, limpjesa   **cleaning / cleanliness**

Muchos productos de limpieza son dañinos para el medio ambiente. ▸ Many cleaning products are harmful for the environment.

limpio/a *adj* • limpjo   **clean**

Las flores y los árboles necesitan aire limpio y agua fresca. ▸ Flowers and trees need clean air and fresh water.

lluvia *n, f* • ʎuβja   **rain**

Los ríos se inundaron con la lluvia torrencial. ▸ The rivers were flooded by the heavy rain.

malgastar *v* • malgastar   **to waste**

Aquí está prohibido malgastar el agua. ▸ It's illegal to waste water here.

mamífero/a *adj* • mamIfeɾoPerez   **mammal**

La ballena no es un pez, sino un mamífero. ▸ The whale is not a fish but a mammal.

medioambiental *adj* • meðjoambjental   **environmental**

Ese documental acerca de la crisis medioambiental me hizo abrir los ojos. ▸
That documentary about the environmental crisis was a real eye-opener.

mejorar v • mexorar   **to improve**

Es hora de que empecemos a pensar en cómo podemos mejorar la situación.
▸ It's time for us to start thinking about how we can improve the situation.

montaña n, f • montaɲa   **mountain**

Sugiero que visiten algunas aldeas en las montañas. ▸ I suggest that you
visit some villages in the mountains.

monte n, m • monte   **hill / mountain**

¡Mira este monte tan alto! ▸ Look at this high mountain!

moral adj • moral   **moral**

Esta es una cuestión moral. ▸ It is a moral question.

niebla n, f • njeβla   **fog / mist**

Una espesa niebla cubrió el campo. ▸ A thick mist covered the countryside.

nube n, f • nuβe   **cloud**

El sol desapareció tras una nube. ▸ The sun disappeared behind a cloud.

nublado/a adj • nuβlaðo   **cloudy**

Me gustan los días nublados. ▸ I like cloudy days.

objetivo n, m • oβxetiβo   **aim / goal / purpose / target**

Con habilidad y perseverancia es posible alcanzar cualquier objetivo. ▸ With skill and perseverance you can achieve any goal.

oceánico/a *adj* • oθeAniko, oseAniko   **oceanic**

¿Podrías nombrar una zona de clima oceánico? ▸ Could you name a location with oceanic climate?

orgánico/a *adj* • orɣAniko   **organic**

El carbonato de amonio es un compuesto orgánico. ▸ Ammonium carbonate is an organic compound.

organización *n, f* • orɣaniθaθjOn, orɣanisasjOn   **organization**

Esta organización depende completamente de donaciones voluntarias. ▸ This organization relies entirely on voluntary donations.

orilla *n, f* • oriʎa   **riverbank / shore**

Cuando era niño, solía ir a la orilla del mar cada verano. ▸ When I was a child, I used to go to the seashore every summer.

paisaje *n, m* • paisaxe   **landscape / scenery**

Contemplamos fijamente el bello paisaje. ▸ We gazed at the beautiful scenery.

parque nacional *n, m* • parke nasjonal **national park / national reserve**

Debemos conservar los parques naturales. ▸ We should preserve natural parks.

peligro *n, m* • peliɣro   **danger**

Están en peligro de extinción. ▸ They are in danger of extinction.

plantar v • plantar   **to plant**

En marzo el suelo aún sigue muy frío como para plantar algo en el jardín. ▸ In March, the ground is still too cold to plant anything in the garden.

polución n, f • poluθjOn, polusjOn   **pollution**

En su último libro ella habla de la polución. ▸ Her latest book deals with pollution.

prado n, m • praðo   **meadow**

Había un ciervo que andaba por el prado. ▸ There was a deer walking through the meadow.

producción n, f • proðukθjOn, proðuksjOn   **production**

La producción se ha incrementado de forma notable. ▸ Production has remarkably increased.

producir v • proðuθir, proðusir   **to produce**

Mediante la ingeniería genética, el maíz puede producir sus propios pesticidas. ▸ Through genetic engineering, corn can produce its own pesticides.

productivo/a adj • proðuktiβo   **productive**

¿Cómo puedo ser más productiva? ▸ How can I be more productive?

producto n, m • proðukto   **product**

Surgieron muchas preguntas acerca de la calidad del nuevo producto. ▸ Many questions came up about the quality of the new product.

productor/a *n, f/m* • pɾoðuktoɾ — **producer**

Estados Unidos es el productor de queso más grande del mundo. ▸ The United States is the largest producer of cheese in the world.

propuesta *n, f* • pɾopwesta — **proposal / proposition / suggestion**

Esa propuesta suena bastante bien. ▸ That sounds like a fairly good proposal.

protegido/a *adj* • pɾotexiðo — **protected**

El cocodrilo es un animal protegido. ▸ The crocodile is a protected species.

raíz *n, f* • raⅠθ, raⅠs — **root**

La chirivía es una raíz que se emplea como hortaliza. ▸ Parsnip is a root employed as a vegetable.

rama *n, f* • rama — **branch**

Una rama de olivo simboliza la paz. ▸ An olive branch symbolizes peace.

reciclable *adj* • reθiklaβle, resiklaβle — **recyclable**

Sólo trabajamos con materiales reciclables. ▸ We only work with recyclable materials.

reciclaje *n, m* • reθiklaxe, resiklaxe — **recycling**

El reciclaje todavía no es tan común en algunos países. ▸ Recycling is still not that common in some countries.

reciclar *v* • reθiklaɾ, resiklaɾ — **to recycle**

Hemos empezado a <u>reciclar</u> periódicos. ▸ We have started to <u>recycle</u> newspapers.

recoger v • rekoxeɾ   **to collect**

Hay que <u>recoger</u> el correo. ▸ The post has to be <u>collected</u>.

recolectar v • rekolektaɾ   **to harvest**

¿Cuándo tienes intención de <u>recolectar</u> el trigo? ▸ When are you planning to <u>harvest</u> the wheat?

recurso n, m • rekuɾso   **mean / resource**

El agua es un <u>recurso</u> natural de vital importancia. ▸ Water is a natural <u>resource</u> of vital importance.

reducción n, f • reðukθjOn, reðuksjOn   **reduction**

Estamos trabajando mucho por la <u>reducción</u> del carbono. ▸ We are working hard towards carbon <u>reduction</u>.

reducir v • reðuθiɾ, reðusiɾ   **to reduce / to lessen**

Para <u>reducir</u> el riesgo de incendio o descarga eléctrica, no exponga este aparato a la lluvia o humedad. ▸ To <u>reduce</u> the risk of fire or electric shock, do not expose this apparatus to rain or moisture.

regar v • reɣaɾ   **to water**

Tenemos que <u>regar</u> las flores. ▸ We need to <u>water</u> the flowers.

reptil n, m • reptil   **reptile**

Le asustan todos los reptiles. ▸ She is scared of all reptiles.

residuo *n, m* • resiðwo **waste**

¿Cómo podemos reducir los residuos medioambientales? ▸ How can we reduce environmental waste?

respirar *v* • respirar **to breathe**

Yo era incapaz de respirar por el humo. ▸ I was unable to breathe because of the smoke.

reutilizar *v* • reutiliθar, reutilisar **to reuse**

Todos deberíamos reutilizar el plástico. ▸ We should all reuse plastic.

saludable *adj* • saluðaβle **healthy**

La vida en el campo es más saludable que en la ciudad. ▸ Country life is healthier than city life.

sed *n, f* • seð **thirst / to be thirsty**

Ciertos alimentos dan sed. ▸ Some kinds of food make one thirsty.

sembrar *v* • sembrar **to plant / to seed / to sow**

Semillas sin sembrar no crecerán. ▸ Seeds unsown do not grow.

semilla *n, f* • semiʎa **seed**

La semilla está empezando a germinar. ▸ The seed is beginning to germinate.

sierra *n, f* • sjera **mountain range**

Esta mañana dimos un paseo muy agradable por esta parte de la sierra. ▸
This morning we went for a lovely stroll around this part of the mountain.

sombra *n, f* • sombɾa   **shade / shadow**

Se sentaron a la sombra de un árbol. ▸ They sat in the shade of a tree.

sostenibilidad *n, f* • sosteniβiliðað   **sustainability**

Las bicicletas son una herramienta para la sostenibilidad urbana. ▸ Bicycles
are tools for urban sustainability.

sostenible *adj* • sosteniβle   **sustainable**

Malgastar tanto como tú no es sostenible. ▸ Wasting as much as you do is
not sustainable.

terreno *n, m* • tereno   **field / piece of land**

Tom compró un terreno cerca de donde vive Mary. ▸ Tom bought a piece of
land not far from where Mary lives.

trasplantar *v* • trasplantaɾ   **to transplant**

Voy a trasplantar estas flores, esta maceta es demasiado pequeña. ▸ I'm trans-
planting these flowers as this flowerpot is too small.

trigo *n, m* • triɣo   **wheat**

Aquí cultivamos trigo. ▸ We grow wheat here.

tronco *n, m* • troŋko   **trunk**

El árbol tenía el tronco nudoso. ▸ The tree had a knotty trunk.

urbano/a *adj* • urβano   **urban**

Un incremento en el número de coches afectará al entorno <u>urbano</u>. ▸ An increase in the number of cars will affect the <u>urban</u> environment.

valle *n, m* ● baʎe   **valley**

Se esconde un bello <u>valle</u> tras esa colina. ▸ A beautiful <u>valley</u> lies behind the hill.

vegetación *n, f* ● bexetaθjOn, bexetasjOn   **vegetation**

Sólo había algunas manchas de <u>vegetación</u> cerca del río. ▸ There were only a few patches of <u>vegetation</u> near the river.

vegetal *n, m* ● bexetal   **vegetable**

Mi <u>vegetal</u> favorito es la berenjena. ▸ My favorite <u>vegetable</u> is eggplant.

vidrio *n, m* ● biðrjo   **glass**

El papel, el <u>vidrio</u> y el plástico son materiales reciclables. ▸ Paper, <u>glass</u> and plastic are recyclable materials.

zonas verdes *n, f* ● sonas berðes   **green areas**

Hay muchas <u>zonas verdes</u> en esta región. ▸ There are several <u>green areas</u> in this region.

Index

Printed in Great Britain
by Amazon